The **YOU DON'T UNDERSTAND ME** *Journal*

Dr Tara Porter is a Clinical Psychologist and writer. She worked in the NHS for over 25 years in child and adolescent mental health and has her own successful private practice. She is the author of the *Sunday Times* bestselling book, *You Don't Understand Me: The Young Woman's Guide to Life*, which has been translated and published around the world. She writes articles about mental health in journals and the mainstream media and is an Associate Tutor on the doctorate programme for Clinical Psychologists at UCL. She has a special interest in mental health in schools and worked previously at the Anna Freud Centre on their Schools in Mind project.

The YOU DON'T UNDERSTAND ME Journal

A guide to self-knowledge, reflection and growth

DR TARA PORTER

Lagom

First published in the UK by Lagom,
An imprint of Bonnier Books UK
4th Floor, Victoria House,
Bloomsbury Square,
London, WC1B 4DA

Owned by Bonnier Books
Sveavägen 56, Stockholm, Sweden

Paperback – 9781785121708

A CIP catalogue of this book is available from the British Library.

Designed and typeset by Envy Design
Diagrams by Envy Design
Illustrations by Katie Foreman
Epigraphs taken from *You Don't Understand Me* by Dr Tara Porter
Printed and bound by Clays Ltd, Elcograf S.p.A

1 3 5 7 9 10 8 6 4 2

Lagom is an imprint of Bonnier Books UK
www.bonnierbooks.co.uk

For Lally,
my lovely Mum.

CONTENTS

PART ONE: SELF-KNOWLEDGE: YOUR RELATIONSHIPS AND BACKGROUND

PART TWO: SELF-REFLECTION: FEELINGS, THOUGHTS AND BEHAVIOUR

PART THREE: SELF-GROWTH: PUTTING IT ALL TOGETHER

HOW TO USE THIS BOOK

Welcome to *The You Don't Understand Me Journal*! In this book, I have put together a series of exercises and worksheets to help you with three things: self-knowledge, self-reflection and personal growth. Whilst aspects of all three concepts occur throughout the book, they largely map on the three main sections of this book. Thus, in Part 1, through thinking about your earlier life, family and relationships you will develop self-knowledge. In Part 2, we move into the self-reflection about your thoughts, feelings, body and behaviour. Finally, in Part 3, we put it all together which allow us to compassionately think about change and self-growth.

This has been designed to mirror the therapeutic journey that I often take with my patients. We talk about their background and relationships, they get to reflect on themselves and then they think about change. I think the book will be most helpful to you if you move through it in order, but of course you are welcome to dip in and out as you choose. Also, some bits might not be as relevant to you: it has also been written with girls and women from 13–25 years old in mind. That's quite a big age span and everyone is different, so you may want to leave out some bits which aren't as relevant to you.

You can use this journal as a standalone workbook. However, its content is based on the accompanying book, *You Don't Understand Me: The Young Woman's Guide to Life* (referred to from now on as *YDUM*). You can therefore find much more information about each topic in *YDUM*. Where something in this book particularly relates back to *YDUM*, it will be flagged like this with the relevant page number: [*YDUM* pg. xx].

There are certain psychological concepts that run through the book. These include: what your values are; identifying the expectations that are put on you (including by yourself); understanding your own emotional landscape; the importance of gratitude and pride in yourself; and, perhaps most importantly of all, balance. Good mental health depends a lot on balance.

Some of the exercises and quizzes are more for self-knowledge and self-reflection, and are probably things you will only do once. Some of the psychological tips, things to try and worksheets are for self-knowledge and self-reflection but also lend themselves to self-growth. These are more likely to be things you might want to come back to again and again.

- Open-ended questions or unfinished sentences for you to complete, which are followed by respectively a question mark or three dots (...).
- Quizzes or other written exercises. These are the sort of questions that I might ask people who come to see me in therapy to identify potential difficulties or problems. This is not therapy, however, and these are not diagnostic. They are more to give you ideas about areas of difficulty.
- Psychological top tips. These are short summaries (taken from *YDUM*) of what might be helpful for a particular issue. The advice is all based on research and clinical experience.
- 'Things to try'. These are the practical exercises based on psychological research and theory to help you feel better. You may want to return to these again and again.
- Worksheets. These are written exercises that again it may be helpful to return to later, as different issues come up in your life. In some cases you may want to use them daily or multiple times a day, so, for example, there is a sleep worksheet you could use every single night. One of the worksheets, on understanding feelings, I have included in seven times as I think it is an important activity

to do several times for self-knowledge and reflection as you work through the journal, as well as being something you can come back to later. You are welcome to photocopy these worksheets for your own personal use.

TRIGGER WARNING

I hope you enjoy using this workbook and find it helpful, but inevitably when we are talking about serious topics sometimes it can be upsetting. Self-knowledge, self-reflection and growth bring up uncomfortable ideas or difficult memories. In thinking about ourselves, our faults or our weaknesses, it is easy to feel useless or hopeless. Similarly, when you think about difficult situations with family or friends, or about your appearance or schoolwork, you may feel upset. I hope that this book will give you strategies to both cope with these temporary feelings in the short term and the tools to move through them in the medium or longer term. However, in the meantime, please make a commitment here to what you can do if you get upset or anxious.

If I get upset or anxious I could...

- Phone (who?) ....
- Text (who?) ....
- Snap (who?) ....
- In real life, talk to (who?) ....
- Do something nice for myself, like (e.g. have a bath, light a candle, play my favourite song)

  ....

  ....

- Calm myself down by (e.g. going for a walk, breathing deeply, cuddling my pet, looking at the stars)

  ....

  ....

- Change my physical surroundings by (e.g. going to a park, sitting on my balcony, going to be with people)

  ....

- Reach out to an adult I know (e.g. a teacher, therapist, parent, aunt or uncle, neighbour, godparent)

  ....

- Phone or text a helpline (e.g. Childline: 0800 1111; The Mix (under 25s): 0808 808 4994; Samaritans: 116 123)

  ....

- Zone out with (e.g. a bath, yoga, mindfulness, prayer, a nap, sleep, meditation)

  ....

- Do something active (e.g. cycle, walk, run, swim, do an online workout, lift weights)

  ....

PSYCHOLOGICAL TOP TIP

This book is not therapy nor does it take the place of professional healthcare. I am giving generic advice, but generic does not suit or help everyone. A workbook requires an active engagement in the process of change and taking self-responsibility, but sometimes mental health problems are too strong, too disabling and too all-encompassing for people to be able to do that. There is no blame and no shame if that is the case for you. Get professional help either through your GP, through your school or university counselling or through mental health services.

INTRODUCTION

My hope is that this book will help you to understand yourself better. I want to help you get to know yourself, reflect on yourself and to grow from where you are – and to help you do these three things through the light of compassion.

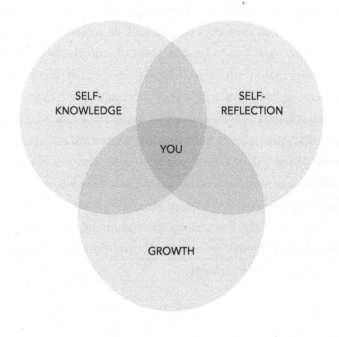

Compassionate self-knowledge

How well do you really know yourself?

- Maybe you feel you know yourself all too well. You may even feel a bit fed up with yourself.
- Perhaps your self-knowledge gets lost as you spend way too much time thinking about what other people are thinking about you.
- Maybe you do a lot of self-deprecation; it can become almost a competitive sport among groups of girls and women to say: 'No, I'm going to do the worst; I am awful compared to you; you are so much better than me.'

But **compassionate self-knowledge** is different from all of these. In this book, I want to encourage you to look at yourself in another way: I want to encourage you to look at yourself *realistically but kindly*. To do this means that you have to acknowledge your strengths as well as your weaknesses; that you accept your successes as well as your failures. I see compassionate self-knowledge as being on a continuum halfway between self-deprecation or fault-seeking at one end, and arrogance and narcissism at the other. Often, young people who self-deprecate and fault-seek have a negative, critical voice constantly harping on in their head (often in the misguided hope of generating humility or motivation). At the other end of the continuum, narcissism and arrogance are when someone admires themselves excessively and they have no capacity to see or accept any self-knowledge.

It is not good to be at either extreme on this continuum in terms of your mental health or your life success. I want you to be in the middle. Please mark where you see yourself on this continuum. I hope this book will help you move towards the middle, which is self-compassion.

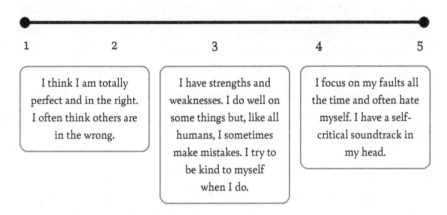

| 1 | 2 | 3 | 4 | 5 |

| I think I am totally perfect and in the right. I often think others are in the wrong. | I have strengths and weaknesses. I do well on some things but, like all humans, I sometimes make mistakes. I try to be kind to myself when I do. | I focus on my faults all the time and often hate myself. I have a self-critical soundtrack in my head. |

Compassionate self-reflection

Once you've had a kindly but accurate look at yourself, I will encourage you to self-reflect – this is really the crux of understanding yourself.

Self-reflection acknowledges the impact of both nature and nurture on who you are today.

- Nature is what you are genetically, which may be unalterable (like your basic body type) or a tendency (like some aspects of personality).
- Nurture is the way you were raised and how your early experiences have shaped you; I sometimes think of this as how you have been wired. Your family obviously has a big impact on this, but so do

your friends, your school, and the community and society in which you have been raised.

Nature and nurture interact with each other, with your personality and with your free will in a complex web to create you: your thoughts, feelings, behaviour and physiology.

The first two parts of the book will focus on self-knowledge and self-reflection: about your background (your relationships and the context you were raised) and how you feel (emotionally and in your body), think and behave.

Compassionate personal growth

In the third section of the book, we will be drawing together the understanding you have gained of yourself from the first two sections, to think about the present and future you. In psychology, we call this a 'formulation': it is your 'story' or 'narrative' if you like. It is an understanding of who you are, where you have come from, and how you got here. Understanding 'where you are' gives you a trajectory into the 'what next', and how you are going to get there.

You are a work in progress. In my opinion, everyone should be a work in progress. In life, change is a constant: your age and stage of life; the people around you and the world itself will always be changing. Teenage and early adulthood are full of change: from school to post-school studying and training, and then a job. You will have to grow so you can adapt to this change.

But growth and change are often hard. Why?

- You are not going to be able to change everything. Accepting what you can and can't change is half the battle.
- Trying to change many things at once is like juggling with jelly: hard to hold onto anything. We all have resources – time, money, energy, friends and our own good qualities (hard work or intelligence, for example) – but we only have limited supplies of them. So, the next stage is deciding which of the things that you are able to change are the ones you most want to commit your limited resources to. If you try to change everything at once, it may be that you change nothing. I see too many young people trying to be perfect in every aspect of their life, which drives them crazy.

- Changing habits is tough. Implementing psychological change involves a shift in habitual ways of thinking, feeling or acting. Changing our thoughts is particularly tough: our brain likes regularity and routine as it is a low-effort option. Have you ever come out of your house and taken your usual route to school when you were meant to be going somewhere different? This is your brain working on autopilot, implementing the usual stuff you do.
- Change is hard because it inevitably involves losing how things used to be. Even positive welcome change involves saying goodbye to some old stuff.

Finally, change and growth do <u>not</u> always involve 'doing better or getting more'. Sometimes the change you need to make is to *stop* doing something. Many unhappy and anxious people I see in therapy are striving for some notion of 'better or more'. But personal growth can be about letting go of expectations (yours or other people's): doing less and enjoying life more. There is often something people need to do less of.

THE THINGS I WANT TO CHANGE ABOUT MYSELF AND MY LIFE

You may have some initial ideas about what you want to change already. Make a note of them here but keep your mind open about this.

....

....

....

....

....

....

....

....

....

....

....

....

....

....

....

....

....

....

COMPASSION

It will not have escaped your notice that the three goals for this book are all underpinned by compassion. Why? Because compassion is both kind and effective.

I spend a lot of my life as a therapist encouraging people to be compassionate about themselves. Maybe you think that is because I am a kindly therapist type. Well, yes, it's a bit of that. But, more importantly, I encourage compassion because it is **effective**.

There is a false belief that we have to be harsh on ourselves to achieve change or be our best self. There is no evidence for that in research or in my clinical practice.

When people are harsh on themselves, they tend to go to extremes: they rubbish **everything** they do. They tell themselves that they will **never** achieve, that they are **completely useless**. These are **absolutes** – they leave no wiggle room. These negative, global judgements do not motivate anyone, because if you are completely useless, where's the room for change? For growth? It's decided already! Absolute judgements make people want to give up; punish themselves or self-sabotage. This sort of harshness paralyses people into inaction through sadness, worry or anger.

But also, they don't allow the **understanding** that self-knowledge and self-reflection bring. When we understand what led us to think, feel or behave the way we did, it opens up opportunities for change and difference in the future. We understand what led us to do that in the past so we can change those things in the future.

Just telling ourselves how awful we are – that we are greedy, stupid, lazy – takes us nowhere except into misery. Facing our faults honestly, but kindly, allows us to address them: 'I really messed up that test; I didn't work hard enough. But I was really too tired to study; it had been a tough week and I was distracted by Netflix. Next time, I'll take care of my sleep better so that I am less tired.'

Are you too harsh on yourself?

I want you to look back to the changes you said you wanted to make in 'The things I want to change about myself and my life' activity.

Did you make global, absolute judgements about yourself? For example, did you write that you wanted to change 'everything' or that you wanted to stop being 'a horrible person' or 'lazy'? This would be one sign that you tend towards this sort of critical thinking.

So, forget about being kind for a moment, and let's focus on effective. *I don't think you will change anything if you don't commit to changing this way of thinking about yourself.* Doing the work on self-knowledge and self-reflection to really understand how and why you do what you do will help with that. If you have made these global, negative judgements in your list of changes, go back, cross out and change them. Don't worry that it looks messy – life is messy, change is messy. Or do a second draft on the next page.

We all need to change stuff, and that will involve crossing out and starting again, or doing new drafts. It doesn't have to look perfect, because it is a sign of something more important: that you are working on your inside.

THE THINGS I WANT TO CHANGE ABOUT MYSELF
AND MY LIFE – SECOND DRAFT

Compassionately, and avoiding negative, global judgements about myself, what do I want to change about myself or my life?

....

....

....

....

....

....

....

....

....

....

....

....

....

....

....

....

....

WHO YOU ARE NOW

My name is ....

I was born in ....

I am .... years old.

I live with ....

My family are ....

....

....

I currently study/work at (school, university, work)
....

My friends are ....

....

....

I am in a relationship with ....

....

....

JUST THREE WORDS TO DESCRIBE ME

I am in three feelings: ....

....

....

....

I am in three personality characteristics: ....

....

....

....

I am interested in three things: ....

....

....

....

Three things I value about myself are: ....

....

....

....

....

15

I HOPE...

For today: ....

....

....

For this month: ....

....

....

For this year: ....

....

....

For next year: ....

....

....

In five years: ....

....

....

MY LIKES AND DISLIKES

I like: ....

....

....

I dislike: ....

....

....

I love: ....

....

....

I hate: ....

....

....

VALUES

A lot of the time, people are encouraging you to think about your goals and outcomes, such as passing a test or exam, getting into college, making the grade. Values are a different way to think about your life: they are about how you want to live, rather than what you want to achieve. The journey rather than the final destination. They are important as they often give satisfaction in the present, as you are living how you want to live, and thus give meaning to your life. As you go through life, you may find different values are important to you at different stages. Choose five values from the list below that are currently important to you. This isn't an exhaustive list, there are some blank spaces at the end to add your own.

Academic achievement		Admiration	
Adventure		Ambition	
Authenticity		Belonging	
Career		Caring/ self-care	
Compassion		Competition	
Confidence		Connection	
Contentment		Control	
Creativity		Curiosity	
Diversity		Environment	
Equality		Excellence	
Faith		Family	
Financial stability		Freedom	

Friendship		Fun	
Gratitude		Health and Fitness	
Home		Honesty	
Hope		Humour	
Inclusion		Independence	
Industry		Integrity	
Intimacy		Joy	
Kindness		Leisure	
Love		Making a difference	
Mindfulness		Nature	
Openness		Optimism	
Order		Peace	
Persistence and commitment		Power	
Pride		Responsibility	
Risk-taking		Safety	
Self-discipline		Sportsmanship	
Success		Trustworthy	
Uniqueness		Work–life balance	

PART ONE

SELF-KNOWLEDGE: YOUR RELATIONSHIPS AND BACKGROUND

CHAPTER 1

YOUR FAMILY

'The journey into your own psychology starts with what
happened to you as a baby. You may not consciously remember it,
but believe me, your first days and months run right through you,
like the writing runs through a stick of rock candy. What happened
to you then, in your first relationships, is imprinted in your brain.
As you grew, it fundamentally shaped you. It's powerful stuff
and worth understanding.'

In this first chapter, I invite you to reflect on the roots of the person you
are today.

I will be inviting you to think about this in two ways. Firstly, about you
in your pre-teen years: your family relationships; your early memories;
the stories that were told to you about you. And secondly, about how
your family relationships are now.

YOUR FAMILY ROOTS

Who you are grows from your roots in your family. On the next page, I want you to draw out who is in your family. Family, of course, includes all your relations who you love and see regularly. But for some of you, it may also include people who haven't shown up for you, or who it is difficult to see because of distance or who have passed away. You may also include people in your family who are not really related to you.

My friends who are like family: ....
....

Pets or animals who feel like family: ....
....

People in paid relationships (such as nannies, childminders)
who feel like family: ....
....

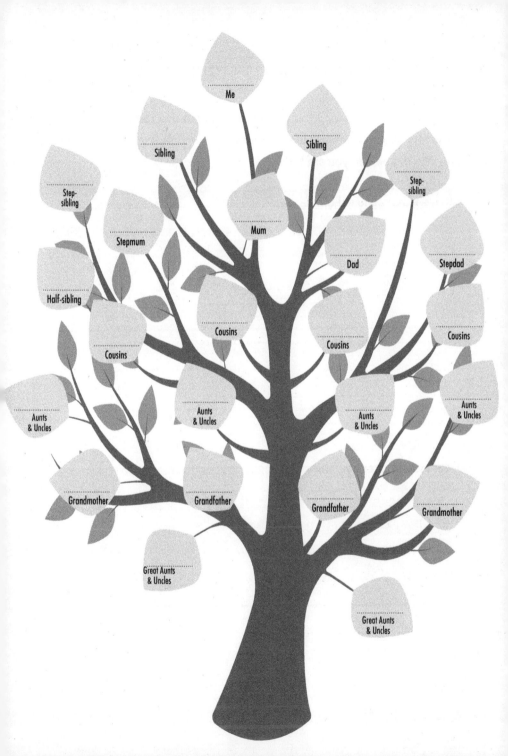

YOU AND YOUR FAMILY IN YOUR EARLY YEARS

In this section I'm inviting you to think about what you remember or have been told about your early life and consider how this might have shaped you into the person you are today.

My birth and early babyhood were: ....

....

....

....

....

....

....

....

....

I was looked after by: ....

....

....

....

....

....

....

....

....

I've been told the following stories about myself as a baby:

....

....

....

....

....

....

My first memories are: ....

....

....

....

....

....

....

....

In my early years, I had other caregivers (e.g. grandparents, aunties or uncles, parents' friends, step-parents, nannies, childminders or babysitters): ....

....

....

....

....

....

What are the best memories of my early life?

....

....

....

....

....

....

What are the worst or unhappiest memories of my early life?

....

....

....

....

....

....

Have I lost anyone important from my family? What was that like for me?

....

....

....

....

....

....

For me, home life was: ....

....

....

....

....

....

....

....

....

....

....

My earliest memories of my sibling(s) are:

....

....

....

....

....

....

....

....

....

....

Our relationship when we were younger was:

....
....
....
....
....
....
....
....
....
....

What was my relationship like with my wider family?

....
....
....
....
....
....
....
....
....
....

RELATIONSHIP WITH PARENTS IN TEENAGE AND POST-TEENAGE YEARS

As they enter teenage life, many young people find themselves growing apart from their parents and there can be more arguments and disagreements. This is not always true, but it can be thought of as an evolutionary way to prepare for being a grown-up and leaving home. Some people find this an easy transition, while others find it more difficult.

Since I turned a teenager, me and my parents are... (Circle those that apply to you; it may be different with each parent, so you could use different colour pens for each parent.)		
Talking more	Talking about the same amount	Talking less
Arguing less than before	Arguing about the same	Arguing more
They know more of my friends	They know the same number of my friends	They know fewer of my friends
Hanging out more	Hanging out with them the same as before	Hanging out with them less
Sharing more interests and hobbies	Continuing to share about the same amount of interests and hobbies	Sharing fewer interests and hobbies
I share more things about my life with them	I share about the same amount of things with them	They know less of what is going on in my life

How do I feel about my closeness with my parents? Is it too much, too little, or just right? ....

....

....

....

If it is too much, what could I do to change that?

....

....

....

If it is too little, what could I do to change that?

....

....

....

Some of the reasons young people don't separate from their parents are listed below. Tick which statements apply to you (you can tick more than one)...

☐ I haven't found my friendship group yet and I hang out with my parents more.

☐ Something bad has happened to me (like bullying, abuse or illness), which has kept me close to my parent(s).

☐ My parents are anxious about me doing things on my own or I do lots of work and activities that keep us tied together.

☐ I really like my parents and want to hang out with them most of the time.

☐ I feel anxious about leaving my parents and doing things more on my own.

☐ Other (please specify): ....
....

Any other thoughts on separating from your parents? There is no right or wrong thing to do, everyone is different, and this is about whether it is right for you. ....

....

....

....

....

....

....

....

....

....

....

....

....

....

....

PARENTING STYLES

Two areas where we can think about parents' differences are [see *YDUM* pages 45–47]:

1. **How firm they are.** By firmness, I mean whether they have lots of rules and boundaries; oversee or plan your life closely; and are strict about your freedom, manners or academic work.
2. **How kind they are.** By kindness, I mean warmth, affection, interest, love. Do you have a strong sense that they are on your side, are interested in you and do things for you?

1. My parents are where on a firm continuum?

1   2   3   4   5

My parents are/were very firm. I don't/didn't have a great deal of personal freedom and they were strict about my academic work, friends, curfews, drug and alcohol use.	My parents are/were in the middle on firmness. They keep/ kept an overview on my wellbeing, and are/were strict on some stuff, but generally OK.	My parents are/were not strict at all. I have/had a great deal of personal freedom and decide(d) for myself about work, friends, what time I came home, drug and alcohol use.

2. Where are my parents on a kind continuum?

1   2   3   4   5

My parents are not very warm and affectionate. I've always felt a distance between them and me. They don't hug or kiss me much and are not really that interested in me as a person.	My parents are in the middle on warmth. They are generally affectionate and kind to me. I have a sense of them being on my side.	My parents are super kind and affectionate, and very interested in everything I do. I feel like I am the centre of their world, and they will do anything for me.

How do/did I find my parents' level of firmness?

....
....
....
....
....
....
....
....
....

How do/did I find my parents' level of kindness? Did how they show affection match how I wanted affection?

....
....
....
....
....
....
....
....
....
....

PARENTAL AUTHORITY AND EXPECTATIONS

PSYCHOLOGICAL TOP TIP

Expectations, what you or other people think should happen in the future, play an important role in our mental health. Mo Gawdat, a famous author and founder of One Billion Happy, argues that our happiness at any moment is greater or equal to our current reality minus our prior expectations. That means that having too high expectations may undermine our happiness.

Expectations can be explicit, which means they are out in the open and spoken, or they can be implicit, which means they are never spoken about. Implicit expectations can be more difficult, insidious even, because you might not notice them or be able to disagree with them if they are never spoken about. Expectations generally start with our parents, but also show up in our other relationships. Crucially, too high expectations can become embedded in your own thinking, where they can wreak havoc on your happiness. So many people I see in therapy have internalised relentless, unrealistic expectations for themselves, which are making them utterly miserable.

What rules or expectations did my parents have? *(Rules are explicit expectations which can be voiced, e.g. that everyone helps with clearing up, or comes to Friday night supper.)* ....

....

....

....

....

....

....

....

....

Are there particular areas where we agree(d) or disagree(d)? *(For example, safety, appearance, money, academics, chores or moral issues.)*

....

....

....

....

....

....

....

....

....

....

What implicit expectations do I feel there are? *(These are the sort of hidden rules or expectations which no one says but guide family behaviour, e.g. that people do (or don't) talk about their feelings or that you are expected to achieve academically.)*

....

....

....

....

....

....

....

....

Are there mismatches in what I wanted and what my parents expect?

....

....

....

....

....

....

....

....

....

How do I feel about the expectations on me? Are there any I'd like
to let go of? ....
....
....
....
....
....
....
....
....
....
....
....
....
....
....
....
....
....
....
....
....
....
....

FAMILY VALUES

What values do you think your parents hold? Looking at the list overleaf, pick out five values that you think each of your parents has communicated to you is important. It is kind of irrelevant which they would choose; what is important is what they have shown you in word or deed.

Academic achievement		Admiration	
Adventure		Ambition	
Authenticity		Belonging	
Career		Caring/self-care	
Compassion		Competition	
Confidence		Connection	
Contentment		Control	
Creativity		Curiosity	
Diversity		Environment	
Equality		Excellence	
Faith		Family	
Financial stability		Freedom	
Friendship		Fun	
Gratitude		Health and Fitness	
Home		Honesty	
Hope		Humour	
Inclusion		Independence	

Industry		Integrity	
Intimacy		Joy	
Kindness		Leisure	
Love		Making a difference	
Mindfulness		Nature	
Openness		Optimism	
Order		Peace	
Persistence and commitment		Power	
Pride		Responsibility	
Risk-taking		Safety	
Self-discipline		Sportsmanship	
Success		Trustworthy	
Uniqueness		Work–life balance	

Looking at my parents' values, are they the same or different from my own values (see page 18)? ....

....

....

....

SIBLINGS

Am I compared to my sibling(s) by other people a lot / not much / not at all? What impact, if any, does that have on me?

....
....
....
....
....
....
....
....
....

Do I compare myself to my sibling(s)? If so, how?

....
....
....
....
....
....
....
....
....

I wonder how you answered the question above. Particularly whether you tend to compare yourself to your siblings in a way that is extreme, e.g. seeing your sibling as useless and awful *or* seeing them as wonderful and that you'll never be as good as them. Sometimes that is because you are projecting your own faults into your sibling [see *YDUM* page 58]. If you answered like this, have another go at answering it. Compare yourself in a more accurate and helpful way, being compassionate to yourself and them.

If I'm being more compassionate and honest, I would compare myself to my sibling(s) in the following ways: ....

....

....

....

....

....

....

....

....

....

....

....

....

Do I have any difficult feelings towards my sibling(s) such as jealousy or resentment? ....

....

....

....

....

....

Do I want my relationship(s) with my sibling(s) to improve, or am I happy with them as they are? ....

....

....

....

....

....

....

If I want our relationship to change, is there anything I need to do to help that?

....

....

....

....

....

....

FAMILY TREE REVISITED

Use the family tree on the next page to track the relationship bonds now rather than your blood relationships. Firstly, fill in the people you included in your first family tree on page 25, and then add the lines. You get to define the lines: they might be anything you want them to be. For example, who are you closest to? Who do you talk to? Who do you share interests with? Who are you similar to? Different from? Who do you share values with? Who has expectations of you? Who inspires you and who would you like to move further away from?

Friends who are like family: ....

....

....

....

Pets or animals who feel like family: ....

....

....

....

People in paid relationships (such as nannies, childminders) who feel like family: ....

....

....

....

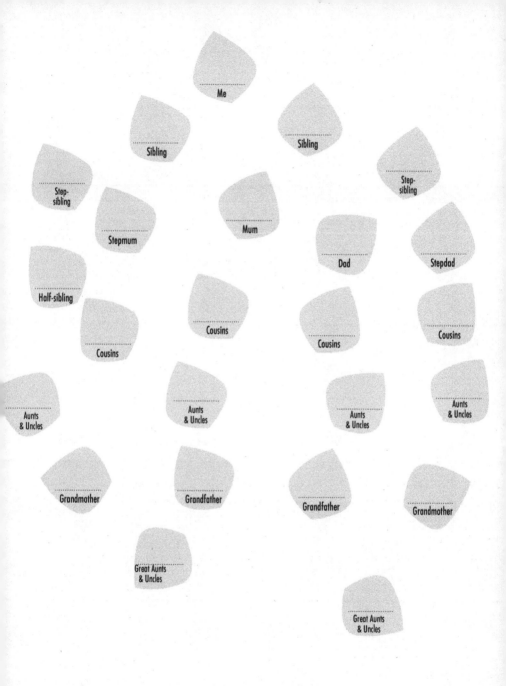

CHAPTER 2

FRIENDS

'Female friendship is deep, complex and intense. As such,
it is often painful and heart-wrenching in childhood but through
adolescence often grows into one of the most important and
beautiful parts of life.'

In this chapter, the focus will be on how your history of friendship and
your current friendships shape you. I will be inviting you to think about
your patterns in friendship, where they came from, and whether they
serve you well now. We will be considering the problem of overthinking
friendships, which is something I see a lot.

PSYCHOLOGICAL TOP TIP

Three ways you can feel in your friendships are:

- A sense of 'belonging'. This is when you feel a sense of acceptance in a group and can be your true self. There are still sometimes disagreements or difficulties, but you are accepted for who you are.
- As though you are 'fitting in'. This is when you have to adjust yourself to fit the majority. When you are fitting in, you feel anxious about showing your true self as you fear exclusion.
- Outside of a friendship group. You may have been rejected or excluded from the group (which is incredibly painful); or you may have chosen not to 'fit in' with a group you don't really 'belong in' and go it alone. E.g. you may just be between friendship groups when they mix up classes in school, or in a gap year when many of your friends have moved away.

When I was very little, I had the following friendships that my parents arranged…

....

....

....

....

....

....

I had the following friendships in primary school...

....

....

....

....

....

....

....

....

....

....

Did I have other important friendships perhaps in my local area or
through hobbies and interests? ....

....

....

....

....

....

....

....

....

....

Did I experience any friendship difficulties in my early life such as an on-and-off friend, or being left out? ....

....

....

....

....

....

....

....

....

....

Did I experience any bullying in my early life?

....

....

....

....

....

....

....

....

....

....

How have these early friendships impacted or influenced me?

....
....
....
....
....
....
....
....
....
....
....
....
....
....
....
....
....
....
....
....
....
....
....

YOUR FRIENDSHIP GROUPS

Friendships can be represented by a Venn diagram pattern with you at the centre. There might be many more than three groups, but they would look something like this:

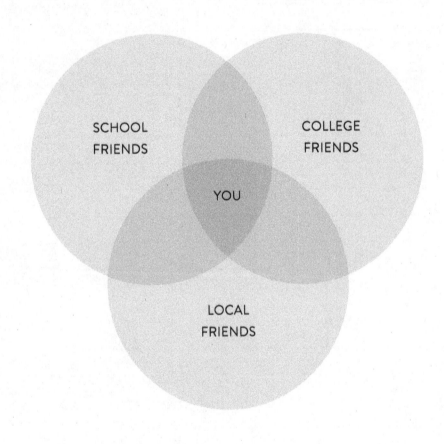

Sometimes there are groups that don't overlap, and particularly after you've turned 18, when you are likely to be working or at university or college. Or there can be an odd one-off friend who doesn't overlap with any other friends. Or you might feel excluded from a group, who may (or may not) be still close with your other friends:

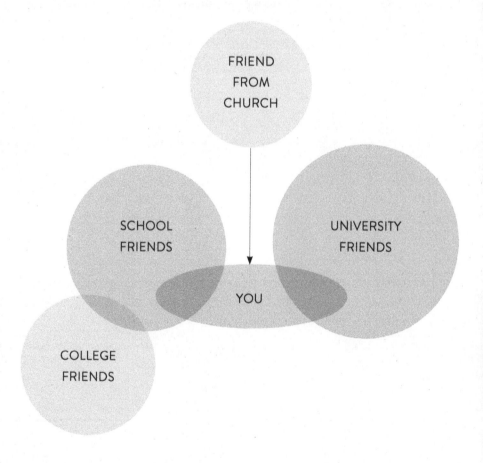

Can you draw out your own friendship groups in a similar style in the space below?

EXPECTATIONS AND VALUES

Do my friendship groups hold any expectations within them? *(Remember from page 37, expectations can be explicit or implicit.)*

....

....

....

....

....

....

....

....

....

....

....

....

....

....

....

....

....

....

What values do my friends have? Do I share these, or do they clash with me or mine? ....

....

....

....

....

....

....

....

....

....

....

....

....

....

....

....

....

....

....

....

....

....

....

....

FRIENDSHIP PATTERNS

PSYCHOLOGICAL TOP TIP

In high school settings, being 'popular' and being 'liked' seem to be separate concepts. Popular kids tend to be cool, smart, pretty or sometimes a bit mean – they hold social power, but are sometimes not well liked. Liked kids can be cool, smart, etc., but more importantly are easy-going, fun, kind and non-hierarchical.

What am I looking for in friendship? Do I prefer to just have one best friend, or a big group? Or to flit from group to group?

....

....

....

....

....

....

....

....

....

....

....

....

....

What qualities do I value in my friends? Do I seek fun more or loyalty?

....
....
....
....
....
....
....
....
....

Am I the friend I want to be? What qualities do I offer in my friendships?

....
....
....
....
....
....
....
....
....
....
....

Do I value popularity or being liked? Is that making me happy?

....
....
....
....
....
....
....
....
....
....

Do I tend to chase friendships or groups that don't particularly want me?
Why do I do that? ....
....
....
....
....
....
....
....
....
....
....

Am I happy with my friendships, or am I looking for something different? Is there anything I can do about that? ....

....

....

....

....

....

....

....

....

OVERTHINKING FRIENDSHIPS

I see a lot of young people who overthink friendships and particularly what their friends think of them. Might this be a problem for you? You may already know, but if not, this quiz will give you some clues.

	Never 1	Occasionally 2	Sometimes 3	Often 3	Nearly always 5
When I am talking to people, I can't really listen to what they are saying because I am thinking about what they are thinking about me.					
After I've been with people, I worry about things I've said and done.					
I often seek reassurance from people after meeting up with them.					
I sometimes avoid social situations because I am anxious.					
I try to control social situations because I am worried about them.					
I feel like I don't know what to say when I am with people.					

PSYCHOLOGICAL TOP TIP

If you got lots of 4s and 5s in this question, it seems that you might be overthinking your friendships. This is likely to make you unhappy for many reasons.

- How you are perceived is mostly a function of the other person's mind, which is, for example, why half of America think Donald Trump is an egotistical crook, and the other half think he is their saviour. Everyone is different and will have a different take on what you do.
- If you are preoccupied with what people are thinking about you, you are not really thinking about them: their feelings, their interests, their concerns. You are not being empathic to their mindset, as you are preoccupied by yours. Thus, your overthinking is taking you away from who you want to be, which is a thoughtful friend.
- Overthinking causes anxiety about socialising, which creates a Catch-22 situation as the anxiety makes the socialising more difficult or awkward, giving you more to overthink.

Am I overthinking friendships? ....

....

....

....

If yes, what could I do about this? ....

....

....

....

....

....

....

....

....

....

....

....

....

....

....

....

PSYCHOLOGICAL TOP TIP

YDUM has some tips about this on pages 83–86, but long answer short: try to think about all the other things that might be on the other person's mind and then connect with those. Their life is much bigger than just you, and a good idea in conversation is to try to discover what they are actually thinking about rather than you.

CHAPTER 3

OTHER RELATIONSHIPS

'There is a myriad of interactions between you and the rest of the society within which you live, work and play. You and your family will be influenced by decisions made and the culture of the society or community within which you live. Similarly, schools have particular styles and expectations, as do the way your peer group acts and the friendship group you fall into.'

Your psychology is not only influenced by your close relationships with family and friends, but also by your relationships with your school, university, community and society as a whole. Attitudes and ideas around you in these contexts may impact on you, for better or for worse. They may affect your growing sense of identity – your sense of who you are and where you fit in the world. This might also include how the world around you reacts to aspects of your culture, race, religion, gender and sexuality. In this chapter, you can reflect on these aspects of you.

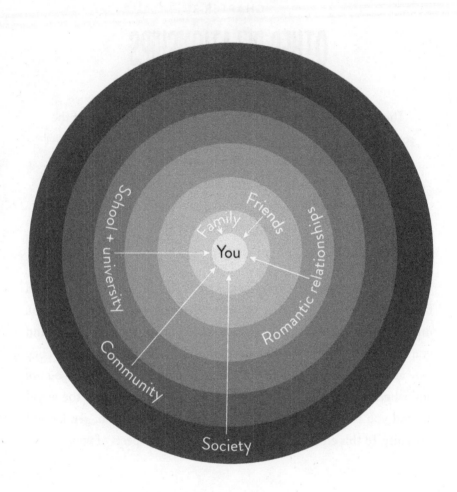

EDUCATION AND SCHOOLS

My primary school was... (For example, did you enjoy it? Did things that happen there still impact on you? How did you feel when you were there?)

....

....

....

....

....

....

....

My secondary transfer was... (For some people this is a really difficult time. How was it for you?) ....

....

....

....

....

....

....

....

....

....

My secondary school suits/suited me because...

....

....

....

....

....

....

....

....

....

....

It didn't suit me because... ....

....

....

....

....

....

....

....

....

....

If relevant, my university/college transfer was... *(For example, did you get your choice of university/college; was it an easy or stressful choice and transfer?)* ....

....

....

....

....

....

....

....

....

University/college is/was... ....

....

....

....

....

....

....

....

....

....

Have I felt academic pressure in school, college or university?

....
....
....
....
....
....
....
....
....
....
....
....
....
....
....
....
....
....
....
....
....
....
....
....

COMMUNITY

Do I feel part of a local community? (*For example, with neighbours; through school, activities or hobbies; through church, race or culture?*)

....

....

....

....

....

....

....

....

Do I feel alienated or excluded by my local community? Have I experienced racism, sexism or any other kind of prejudice in my day-to-day life? ....

....

....

....

....

....

....

....

....

Am I part of any other communities or online communities to do with my own interests or identity? ....

....

....

....

....

....

....

....

....

....

Do the values or expectations of my communities match my own?

....

....

....

....

....

....

....

....

....

SOCIETY

How am I influenced or impacted by my, or my family's, country of origin? Or the current country I live in?

....
....
....
....
....
....
....
....
....

Have world events, like wars or Covid, impacted on me?

....
....
....
....
....
....
....
....
....
....

Am I influenced by political movements like feminism or climate change?

....
....
....
....
....
....
....
....
....

Do I feel any expectations in relation to cultural norms or standards? Do I tend to react towards conformity or rebel against these?

....
....
....
....
....
....
....
....
....
....
....
....

ROMANCE AND SEXUALITY

In terms of liking people, getting with people, sex and romance, my history is... ....

....

....

....

....

....

....

....

The gender and sexuality I identify with is...

....

....

....

....

....

....

....

....

....

....

Do I have any patterns in romantic/sexual relationships? For example, do I shy away or come on too strong, go for people who don't like me, get too committed too quickly or shy away from commitment?

....
....
....
....
....
....
....
....

What are my values in romantic and sexual relationships? Do I believe in one partner at a time, or do I want to get with a lot of partners? Or am I more romantic or sentimental? ....

....
....
....
....
....
....
....
....

Do I feel / have I felt any expectations on me in romance or sex to be or behave in a particular way? ....

....

....

....

....

....

....

....

....

....

Have my values and expectations matched those of the people I've got with? ....

....

....

....

....

....

....

....

....

....

....

Has anything bad happened in romantic relationships, particularly being forced or coerced, but also shamed, which may influence my future relationships? ....

....

....

....

....

....

....

....

....

....

....

....

....

....

....

....

....

....

....

....

....

....

FINISHING PART ONE: YOUR RELATIONSHIPS AND YOUR BACKGROUND

As you finish this part of the book, I invite you to reflect on what you have learnt by completing it. Did anything surprise you about your relationships and background that you hadn't realised before? Is there anything you want to take forward to think about more in the rest of the book that you think is really important? Or is there stuff you want to leave behind here, that you don't want to think about any more? Has anything new emerged that you now want to change?

....

....

....

....

....

....

....

....

....

....

....

....

....

....

SELF-REFLECTION: FEELINGS, THOUGHTS AND BEHAVIOUR

CHAPTER 4

FEELINGS AND EMOTIONS

'You want to aim for emotional competence ... [that] you are aware of your feelings, able to identify and name them, and you manage these to your best advantage to have a happy and fulfilling life, while being sensitive to, but not overwhelmed by, the feelings of others.'

Feelings and emotions are at the centre of self-knowledge, self-reflection and personal growth. We are aiming for emotional competence: to be able to truly allow your feelings, to neither be floored by them nor dominated by them, while still keeping in mind the feelings of others. So, in this chapter, we will be trying to understand how your own feelings work. That starts with naming your feelings, and knowing which of them show up regularly for you, and in what relationships or situations, i.e. 'what triggers you'. Then, there are some worksheets that are designed to help you break feelings into their composite components (which are body, behaviour and thinking). In the following two chapters, we will continue this process of making links between your feelings, your body and your behaviour (Chapter 5), and then to your thinking (Chapter 6).

NAMING YOUR FEELINGS

Being able to accurately name your feelings – at least to yourself but ideally to other people too – will help build your emotional competence. Giving a name to a feeling can provide an instant relief, an acceptance. In my therapy room, I often use a feelings wheel to help people do this. With a feelings wheel, you can start in the centre to identify which broad emotions you are feeling, and then move out to the next layer, and finally the third to find more nuanced words to capture your experience. Sometimes our feelings are not neat, and don't fall into one category. I'm putting them into broad categories to help the process of identifying, but actually the reality is often more messy. We can often feel things which are quite opposite about the same thing.

Practise using the feelings wheel opposite to tune in to your feelings with the next set of questions:

Which of the 7 central emotions most captures how I am feeling right now?

....

....

What about the feelings on the next layer?

....

....

And the next layer?

....

....

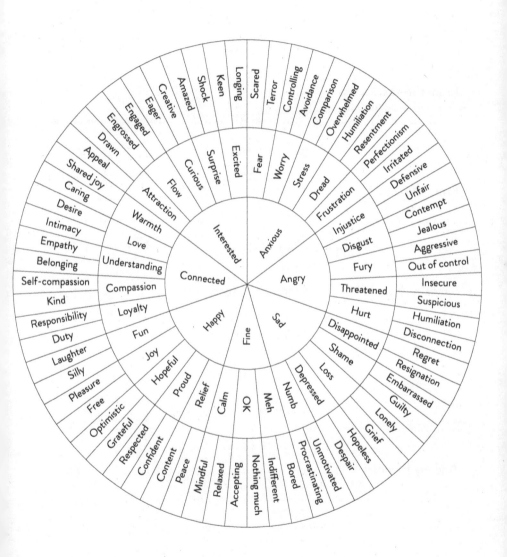

What do I generally feel on a day-to-day basis? From the centre?

....

....

From the next layer?

....

....

From the third layer?

....

....

Similarly, how do I generally feel about my family? ....

....

....

....

....

....

And my friends? ....

....

....

....

....

....

What do I feel about my current romantic/sexual relationships?

....
....
....
....
....
....
....
....
....
....

What about any past romantic/sexual relationships?

....
....
....
....
....
....
....
....
....
....

Where do I go with negative feelings? To sadness? Anxiety? Anger?
(In my experience, people can channel all their negative feelings through one
more than the other two.) ....

....

....

....

Why do I think this is? ....

....

....

....

....

....

....

....

....

....

....

....

....

....

....

....

PSYCHOLOGICAL TOP TIP

Your feelings are often sparked by something outside of you: they are often triggered by life, but you experience them through your body and your mind. We could represent it like this:

Your feelings = the context/life event + your bodily reaction + your thinking

Certain acute or chronic life events, like the death of someone close to you, would have a strong emotional impact on nearly everyone. Other life events are more idiosyncratic, in that they may affect you but not other people. Understanding what affects you can be important in understanding your own emotional life.

Looking back on my life, what acute life events did I have strong feelings about? What feelings were they? (*Acute life events are short or shocking life events that happened once or twice, such as a death or birth, an accident or a wonderful surprise.*)

....

....

....

....

....

....

....

....

What chronic life events did/do I have strong feelings about? What feelings were they? (*Chronic life events are long-term, ongoing things like poverty, unemployment, disability.*)

....

....

....

....

....

....

....

....

....

How do I feel about those events now? Do they still have an emotional impact on me? Might similar events trigger me in the future?

....
....
....
....
....
....
....
....
....
....
....
....
....
....
....
....
....
....
....
....
....
....

THINGS TO TRY: WHEN LIFE EVENTS
KNOCK YOU SIDEWAYS

THINGS TO TRY: RIDE THE WAVE

Sometimes when feelings come, they can feel overwhelming, like a wave trying to knock you to the ground. When you feel overwhelmed with feelings, take a moment to sit down, shut your eyes, and experience the feeling as a big wave. It is threatening to subsume you at the moment, but you know **feelings like waves come and go**. You just have to wait until it passes.

Sit with the feeling 'wave' for a moment and think about what you can do to help you cope with this wave until it fades away... Think of this like surfing the wave. It's not

going to subsume you; you can't stop the wave but think about what you can do that makes you feel better, so you can surf over it.

I can surf the wave of my difficult feelings by...

....

....

....

....

....

....

....

....

....

....

....

....

....

....

....

....

....

....

....

....

CHANGING YOUR PERSPECTIVE

When you are beset by a problem or a worry, write it down briefly on a piece of paper, and hold that piece of paper right in front of your eyes. Stare at the problem: it is right there in front of you, and it is hard to see anything else. Look at it intensely and closely for a moment.

Now move it further away from your face, and try to hold it at a distance with your arms stretched out. How does that feel? Will your arms get tired pushing it away?

What if you put it down on your lap, or next to you on the chair or sofa? What does that feel like? What if you turn it over so you can't see it? Look around further away and look for things that remind you of more positive or happy things you have going on in your life. Your problem has not gone away, it is right there next to you, but just for a few moments, try to think about the non-problem stuff.

MY PROBLEM IS THERE, RESTING BESIDE ME
BUT I WILL THINK ABOUT...

Who do I love? (Person, animal or thing.)

....

....

Who am I loved by?

....

....

What makes me laugh?

....

....

I also like or enjoy (Can I do that right now with my problem beside me?)...

....

....

In the future I am hoping to...

....

....

I'm quite good at...

....

....

PSYCHOLOGICAL TOP TIP

Up to now, in this workbook we have been focusing on how the world outside you (such as your family, community and society and your friends) impacts on you. But YOU impact on you too. Your feelings are linked to three other things about you:

- **Your thoughts.** If you think about something sad that happened in your past or something worrying that is happening in your future, you will likely also feel sad or worry, even though nothing has actually changed from the minute before.
- **Your body.** You get the feeling because your thoughts trigger a hormonal response through your body.
- **Your behaviour.** When you get a feeling, you will likely act in ways that increase or decrease the feeling. Sometimes your behaviour will stop the difficult feeling in the short term but make it worse in the long term.

Your thinking in particular will be key in your emotional reaction. On the next page are two examples from *YDUM*, where thinking differently about the same event – being left alone – leads to a different emotional response in the body and mind.

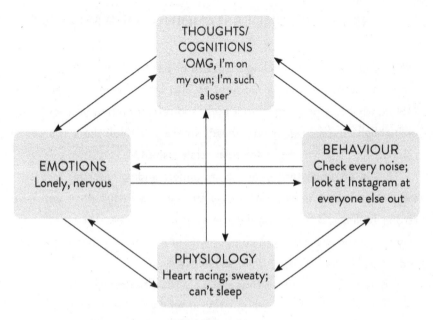

Situation of being left alone in a house on your own

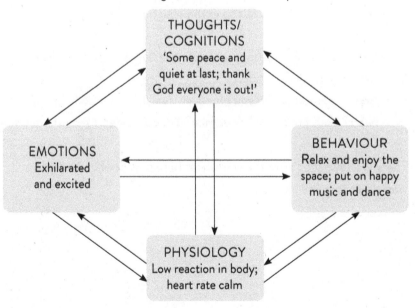

WORKSHEETS: UNDERSTANDING YOUR FEELINGS

When you get a strong feeling (negative or positive) over the next week, record it here, and take a moment to also listen in on your thoughts. Notice what is happening in your body and reflect on how you act. Draw or highlight the arrows or arrowheads where you think there is a causal relationship. You may notice circular relationships.

This is an important exercise in understanding yourself and so I suggest you do it several times over the next few days when you have strong feelings. Briefly describe the external situation. Then work your way round the four different components of emotional experience in any order you like and as many times as necessary.

On each sheet there are four elements to write down:
- Thoughts: Whatever is circulating around your head. Imagine someone was listening to your thoughts. What would they hear?
- Behaviour: What did you do in the situation – before, during, and after?
- Feelings: Use the feelings wheel if necessary to figure out what you were emotionally feeling.
- Bodily sensations: Do you physically feel it in your body? Your heart? Your breathing? Your face? Your shoulders? Anywhere else?

There are seven copies of the worksheet here so it can be used as a worksheet to come back to.

WORKSHEET: UNDERSTANDING MY FEELINGS

Date: ....

External situation: ....

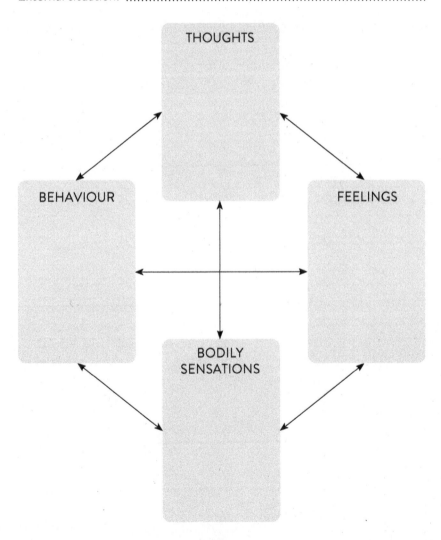

THOUGHTS

BEHAVIOUR

FEELINGS

BODILY
SENSATIONS

WORKSHEET: UNDERSTANDING MY FEELINGS

Date: ....

External situation: ....

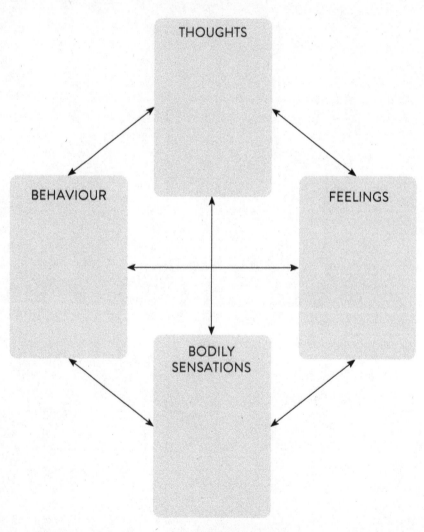

THOUGHTS

BEHAVIOUR

FEELINGS

BODILY
SENSATIONS

WORKSHEET: UNDERSTANDING MY FEELINGS

Date: ....

External situation: ....

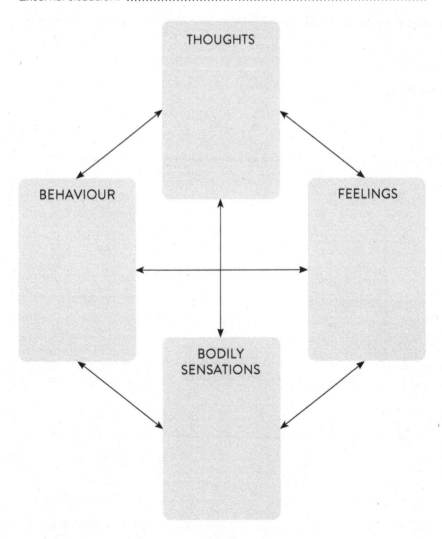

WORKSHEET: UNDERSTANDING MY FEELINGS

Date: ....

External situation: ....

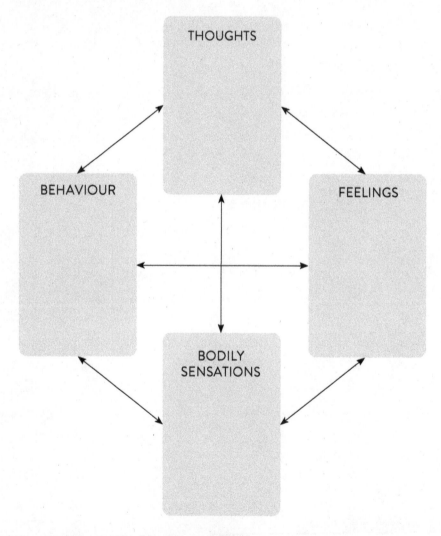

WORKSHEET: UNDERSTANDING MY FEELINGS

Date: ....

External situation: ....

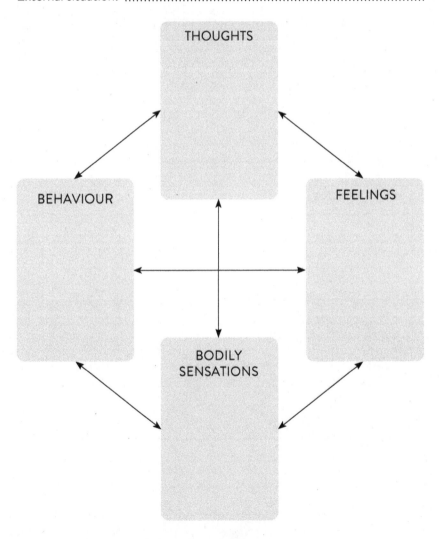

WORKSHEET: UNDERSTANDING MY FEELINGS

Date: ....

External situation: ....

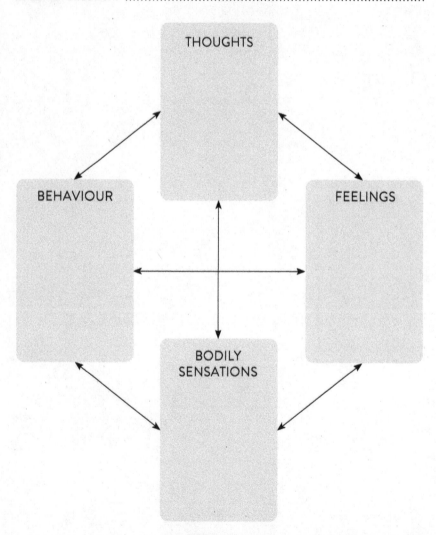

WORKSHEET: UNDERSTANDING MY FEELINGS

Date: ....

External situation: ....

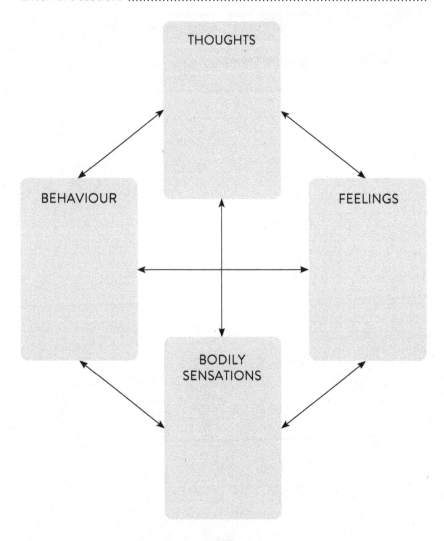

UNDERSTANDING YOUR FEELINGS: REFLECTION

After completing a few or all of these worksheets, look back at them and see what you can learn. It's important to stay compassionate to yourself in this exercise, as you will likely be reflecting on your weaknesses and faults – like every human, you have these too.

1. Reflections on my positive feelings: ....

....

....

....

....

....

....

....

....

....

....

....

....

....

....

....

2. Were they linked to any particular thoughts, behaviours or physical symptoms or states? ....

....

....

....

....

....

....

....

....

....

....

....

....

....

....

....

....

....

....

....

....

....

3. Were they linked to particular situations?

4. Reflections on negative feelings:

....
....
....
....
....
....
....
....
....
....
....
....
....
....
....
....
....
....
....
....
....
....
....
....
....

5. Were they linked to any particular thoughts, behaviours and physical symptoms or states? ....

....

....

....

....

....

....

....

....

....

....

....

....

....

....

....

....

....

....

....

....

....

....

6. Were they linked to any particular situations?

....

....

....

....

....

....

....

....

....

....

....

....

....

....

....

....

....

....

....

....

....

....

END-OF-CHAPTER REFLECTION: FEELINGS AND EMOTIONS

PSYCHOLOGICAL TOP TIP

Feelings can become a problem when:

- You get stuck in them.
- They are out of proportion with what is going on.
- They interfere with daily life.
- They become merged with identity, e.g. I'm just an anxious person.
- They are confused with truth, e.g. because I feel it, it must be true.
- They are used to control others, e.g. you need to do (or stop doing) this, because I feel that...

What have I learnt about my feelings in this chapter?

....

....

....

....

....

....

....

....

....

What would I like to change about my feelings?

....

....

....

....

....

....

....

....

....

....

....

....

....

....

....

....

....

Over the next few chapters, we will be trying to understand your feelings and moods more, and giving you lots of opportunities to improve them. However, if self-care or self-help isn't enough, you may need to get professional help. Your GP or school/university/work mental health services are good places to start looking for that help.

THINGS TO TRY: FEELING BOOSTERS

We'll be working on improving mood through your body, behaviour and thoughts in the next two chapters, but here, list your own short-term mood boosters to try.

List 10 small pleasures that you could enjoy:

1. ....

2. ....

3. ....

4. ....

5. ....

6. ....

7. ....

8. ....

9. ....

10. ....

List your 10 favourite upbeat songs that you could play:

1. ....
2. ....
3. ....
4. ....
5. ....
6. ....
7. ....
8. ....
9. ....
10. ....

List 10 things that make you laugh:

1. ....
2. ....
3. ....
4. ....
5. ....
6. ....
7. ....
8. ....
9. ....
10. ....

List 10 things you are grateful for:

1. ....

2. ....

3. ....

4. ....

5. ....

6. ....

7. ....

8. ....

9. ....

10. ....

CHAPTER 5

UNDERSTANDING HOW YOUR BODY AND BEHAVIOUR IMPACT ON YOUR FEELINGS

'You should not see yourself as a passive victim of external or internal forces: you have the capacity to change your thoughts, behaviour and physiology so that your anxiety is reduced.'

In this chapter we will be thinking about the impact of your body (your physiology) and your behaviour (what you do) on your feelings. We can gain some mastery over feelings through our body and behaviour. Firstly, your body.

THE PHYSICAL COMPONENT OF EMOTIONS

PSYCHOLOGICAL TOP TIP

Our emotions are not separate from our bodies. They exist in our bodies and have the same physical basis as aches and pains. Emotions are linked to nearly every organ in the body, blood flow and hormones. This is a two-way street.

1. Your emotions will show up in your body.
2. Your physical health will show up in your emotions.

Where do my emotions show up in my body?

- ☐ I get headaches
- ☐ I feel jittery
- ☐ I get tummy aches
- ☐ I feel tense
- ☐ I breathe too fast
- ☐ My legs go wobbly
- ☐ My hands clench
- ☐ I need to pee
- ☐ I can feel my heart pounding in my chest
- ☐ I get sweaty
- ☐ I want to sleep

- ☐ I can't sleep
- ☐ I can't eat
- ☐ I feel sick
- ☐ I want to eat
- ☐ I feel light-headed
- ☐ I have a panic attack (extreme hyperventilation that you can't control)
- ☐ I think I am having a heart attack
- ☐ I zone out

What are my self-reflections on how my emotions show up in my body?

....

....

....

....

....

....

....

....

....

....

....

....

....

....

What do I do to manage or reduce these symptoms? Is what I do helpful?

....

....

....

....

....

....

....

....

....

....

....

....

....

....

....

....

Where does my body show up in my emotions? Which of these physiological things impacts on my mood?

- [ ] My period or pre-menstrual
- [ ] Tiredness
- [ ] Hungry
- [ ] Not moving my body
- [ ] Moving my body too much
- [ ] Pain or illness
- [ ] Other ....

How does my physical wellbeing influence my mental wellbeing?

....
....
....
....
....
....
....
....
....
....
....
....

....

....

....

....

....

....

How do I manage that? Is there anything I should be doing more of?

....

....

....

....

....

....

....

....

....

....

....

....

....

....

....

THINGS TO TRY: WAYS TO HELP YOUR BODY/FEELING CONNECTION

PSYCHOLOGICAL TOP TIP

Changing the physiology of your body is one sure-fire way of changing your emotions through the biochemistry of your body. Don't underestimate the power of this: your mind lives in your body and therefore any changes at body level directly impact on mood. If you are feeling intense emotions, changing something about your body tends to change that emotion.

In this next section, there are four different categories of things to try to help yourself regain equanimity when your feelings start going haywire. The four categories focus on breathing, muscle tension, body sensations and body sustenance. I hope you find some of them useful.

THINGS TO TRY: BREATHING

Breathing can be like magic for difficult feelings. When we are upset, we tend to **automatically** breathe in more and faster. But we don't have to let our breathing be on autopilot, we can take **conscious control** of it. Consciously breathing slowly and remembering to breathe out is like sending a DM to the core of your brain: 'You are safe; it's OK; calm it all down.' Your brain then releases different hormones and chemicals as a result. Breathing is not nothing... People tend to think, *Yeah, yeah, breathing – whatever. How is that going to change anything?* But it does: it can literally change the pH balance of the blood, for example. That's not nothing.

Finding the right way for you to breathe slowly-and-out is a matter of trial and error. Here are some ways that other people find helpful:

- Breathe in and out as you run your finger up and down the fingers of the other hand. This can help regulate your breathing.
- Breathe in and out while counting to ten – try to make the in-breath last to 3 or 4 and the out-breath longer to 8 or 9, then pause for 10 before starting again.
- Sit with someone else who is calm and tag your breathing to theirs.
- Put your hand on your tummy and focus on slowing your breathing in and breathing out as your tummy goes up and down.

THINGS TO TRY: MUSCLE TENSION

If breathing is magic, easing muscle tension is like the magician's assistant:

- Shut your eyes, breathe out, and say the word 'relax' calmly and gently to yourself. Say it slowly five times more. Let your shoulders flop down. Notice all the areas of tension in your body and let go of them.
- Practise progressive muscle relaxation exercises or meditation – links given in References and Further Information (page 237).
- Yoga and pilates are classic 'relaxation' style exercises and they work for many people, but I've had patients who have done the opposite and found tension relief through running, spinning, kickboxing, etc. At the end, they feel physically exhausted, and the tension is used up.

THINGS TO TRY: SENSATIONS IN YOUR BODY

Changing the sensations your body is experiencing will force your brain to refocus and process these. Here we are looking at touch, taste, smell, sight and sound:

- It's a bit of a cliché, but a warm bath, a scented candle and wearing soft, comfy, silky clothes works for some.
- Cold water splashed on the face can shock your feelings to rejig.
- Going outside can help, especially when it feels very different to inside (e.g. to feel the rain or sun on your face, or the wind in your hair).
- Dance to your favourite disco beat. Listening to sad music will not change your mood if you are already feeling down – it will

likely compound it. And sometimes that's OK: we all need to feel the pain and grieve sad things. But when you are fed up of being sad or anxious, upbeat music may help you shift out of that feeling.

- A strong smell can be super evocative – an incense stick, essential oils, your favourite perfume.
- Rub your body massage-style. Better yet, get a trusted friend or family member to rub your shoulders or give you a head massage.
- Lie down, wrap yourself in a blanket, listen to a podcast, comedy show or audio book. It can feel like being read a bedtime story.

THINGS TO TRY: SUSTAIN YOUR BODY

Nurturing yourself to provide rest and nutrition will also change your physiology. Hopefully you have had a previous experience of this as a child when your parents took care of you. Heard of the term 'hangry'? Hunger or thirst can really impact on mood, and tiredness more than anything.

- Make yourself a drink: a nice cup of tea, coffee or hot chocolate but in your favourite mug or cup and saucer.
- Make yourself something delicious to eat – something nurturing. Try not to eat chocolate spread out of a jar, or eat mindlessly, as you will likely end up feeling worse. This is about treating yourself well – so by all means make some chocolate spread on toast and eat it slowly listening to music / sitting in the sun / looking out a window / enjoying every mouthful.
- Have a nap or go to bed if it's late. Make it as nice as you can – hot water bottle, eye mask, special hand cream, clean pyjamas.

WHAT DO I DO TO COPE WITH NEGATIVE FEELINGS?

In this exercise we are going to look at some of the good and not-so-good things people do to cope with negative feelings. Just to warn you, thinking about negative coping strategies can be triggering for some people, especially if they used to do them and have since given up.

What do you do in the moment of feeling awful? It may not sometimes feel like it, but you do have a choice about what you do with negative feelings. Below are some of the behavioural and physiological things I see young people do. First, circle all the ones you do. Then, go back and tick the ones which you think are helpful in the long term as well as the short term, and put a cross through the ones that are tempting to do as a short-term fix when you are feeling bad, but are counterproductive in the longer term. Use a question mark if they are sometimes positive and sometimes negative. This exercise includes some very unhelpful things as well as some constructive things. There are also some blank circles for you to fill in other things you do.

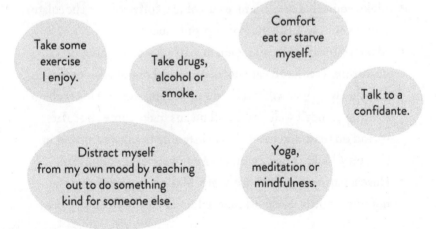

Go for a nap or to bed if it is late.

Doom-scrolling.

Spending time with animals.

Get cross with or be mean to other people.

Moan.

Hurt myself.

Shit talk people behind their back.

Sit outside, go for a walk.

Try to control things and plan.

Distract self with work.

Binge eating and purging/vomiting.

Wallow in either self-justification or self-blame.

Avoid situations.

Moderate social media use for connection and communication.

Reflective journaling.

Distract self with TV.

COPING WITH NEGATIVE FEELINGS: REFLECTION

Reflecting on the previous exercise, what do I notice about how I cope with difficult feelings? Do I mostly use helpful or unhelpful strategies?

....

....

....

....

....

....

....

....

....

....

....

....

....

....

....

....

....

....

Do I ever do things which could be potentially helpful in moderation, but I do them to the extreme? For example, binge-watching a TV show half the night; doom-scrolling for hours; or studying to excess at the expense of sleep? ....

....

....

....

....

....

....

....

....

....

....

....

....

....

....

....

....

....

....

I could try out the following things to see if they help with my feelings...

....
....
....
....
....
....
....
....
....
....
....
....
....
....
....
....
....
....
....
....
....
....
....
....

I could try to cut out or reduce the following unhelpful things...

....

....

....

....

....

....

....

....

....

....

....

....

....

....

PSYCHOLOGICAL TOP TIP

It's so hard to change habits either when you are stopping something or starting something. You will likely fail many times at first and have to start again and again. You will have to repeat the new behaviour many, many times before it becomes habitual itself. Do not be discouraged or too harsh on yourself – this is the just the way humans are.

QUIZ: SCREENS, INTERNET AND SOCIAL MEDIA

One particular behaviour that is linked to mental health is screen use. Take this quiz (if you dare!) to see if this is a potentially a problem for you.

	Never 1	Rarely 2	Some-times 3	Often 3	Always 5
I like to have my phone with me all the time.					
Being on social media or gaming stops me doing the basic things in life like eating, sleeping, exercise or schoolwork.					
I carry on scrolling even though I'm bored or tired.					
I do things online that I would be ashamed for people in real life to know about.					
I find it hard to get off my phone or stop gaming once I've started.					
When I'm on social media I think that other people are better than me.					

	Never 1	Rarely 2	Some-times 3	Often 3	Always 5
I scroll for several hours a day through stuff posted by people I don't know.					
I use my phone to stay in touch with my friends and look stuff up.					
I feel wired after being on my phone.					
I often laugh when I am online.					
I compare myself unfavourably to people I see online.					
I like to be available for my friends online so I don't go to sleep.					

Common problems associated with screens are: being online too much of the time; using screens for comparison; having trouble coming off a screen; using it to look at upsetting content and being overstimulated. If you answered a lot of 4s and 5s, this could be a sign that you might not have the healthiest relationship with your screen. There are two questions which are exceptions to this (8 and 10), which are about healthier reasons to use your screen, including connection and enjoyment.

PSYCHOLOGICAL TOP TIP

Over the next few pages we will go over the foundations of good mental health – the things that are absolutely necessary to have in place before you can feel good – and screen use can undermine all of them. Finding ways to limit the overall number of hours you are on your phone and knowing how to stop scrolling before you lose hours in a day are key to healthy screen use. Many young people use app-blockers to help them. Try to notice the tipping point where screen use changes from positive to negative. For example, when it changes from you connecting to people, to you comparing yourself to people; or when it changes from an enjoyable break from your work to procrastinating; or when it changes from a kind of mindless activity to something which is increasing your anxiety. These tipping points are important as they signal when you should stop and put away your phone.

Do I need to make any changes in my screen use? What are they?

....
....
....
....
....
....
....
....
....

How could I do this? ....
....
....
....
....
....
....
....
....
....

PSYCHOLOGICAL TOP TIP

There are five things which are crucial for good mental health. They are:

- Sleeping enough
- Eating enough
- Moving enough
- Connection
- Reflection and being in the moment

Often, people come to therapy wanting to feel better mentally, but forget that their brain lives in their body and so is subject to similar rules to our physical health. That is, if you don't take care of your body, your mind will suffer. So, three of these cornerstones of mental health (sleeping, eating, moving) are things you do (behaviours) that impact on your physiology. One is social (connection) and only one is psychological (reflection/ being in the moment). All of them need to be in balance, not to be done to extreme: if you do too much or too little of any of them, they can become a problem.

PSYCHOLOGICAL TOP TIP

The quickest way to upset your mood is to deprive yourself of sleep.
Three things are important when going to sleep:

- Being in touch with your bodily (circadian) rhythms. There is a
  window when falling asleep is easier, and once missed, it can be
  harder to fall asleep. Typically, this is around 10:30–11:30pm.
- Being mentally calm. Winding down and not adding more
  stimulation to your brain is important. Your phone is likely a
  stimulant for your brain, where you are taking in new information.
  If you want to sleep well, it is a good idea to do non-stimulating
  stuff before bed. For example, have a bath, potter around your
  room tidying up, meditate, do yoga, pray, read or listen to a book,
  listen to calming music or a podcast. Journaling gratitude and self-
  compassion may also help. There is a worksheet on pages 156–7
  you may like to use.
- Being physically tired is linked to physical activity, access to
  sunlight and caffeine use as well as the number of hours you have
  been awake.

My sleep pattern is...

....

....

....

....

....

Am I getting the right amount of sleep to support my mental health or am I getting too little or too much?

....
....
....
....
....
....
....

My bedtime routine is... ....

....
....
....
....
....
....

I sleep better when... ....

....
....
....
....
....

I sleep worse when... ....

....

....

....

....

....

....

....

....

....

....

I could improve my sleep by... ....

....

....

....

....

....

....

....

....

....

EATING

My eating pattern is… ....
....
....
....
....
....
....
....
....
....
....

Am I generally getting enough food and eating regularly? Or do I restrict myself in the amount of food I eat and feel hungry? (Sometimes this is called dieting!) ....

....

....

....

....

....

....

....

....

....

Do I restrict the type of food I eat? For example, do I avoid certain food types as I believe them to be fattening or unhealthy?

....

....

....

....

....

....

....

....

Am I very influenced in what I eat by ideas of slimness, health, dieting, etc.? ....
....
....
....
....
....
....
....
....
....
....

Do I overeat or comfort eat? When? How? Why?
....
....
....
....
....
....
....
....
....
....

Do I get a balance of protein, carbs and fruit/veg, more or less?

....
....
....
....
....
....
....
....
....
....

What is one thing I could do to improve my eating?

....
....
....
....
....
....
....
....
....

MOVEMENT

Generally, I move my body in the following ways...

....

....

....

....

....

....

Is this enough? Or am I pushing myself too much?

....

....

....

....

....

....

....

What exercise do I enjoy? Is this the same as the exercise I already do?
If not, why not? ....

....

....

....

....

....

....

....

....

If I don't do enough, what exercise or way of moving my body do I think
I might enjoy that I have never tried or used to love but don't do now?
(Remember things like dancing, horse riding and walking in a city are all
still exercise.) ....

....

....

....

....

....

....

....

....

What plan can I make for doing that? ....
....
....
....
....
....
....
....
....
....
....
....
....
....
....
....
....
....
....
....
....

CONNECTION

Do I have friends and family that regularly bring me feelings of being happy or loved? ....

....

....

....

....

....

....

....

....

....

....

....

....

....

....

....

Am I regularly meeting people to have fun and laughter?

....
....
....
....
....
....
....
....
....
....

Do I have friends and family who will show up if I am sad, worried or angry, to listen and support me? ....

....
....
....
....
....
....
....
....
....

....

....

....

....

....

....

Do I seek company too much, and find it hard to be on my own and sit with my own feelings? ....

....

....

....

....

....

....

....

....

....

....

....

....

....

....

REFLECTION AND BEING IN THE MOMENT

As well as this journal, do I spend other time thinking about my thoughts, feelings, behaviour and physiology? (*This could be thinking, talking, therapy, keeping a diary or praying.*)

....

....

....

....

....

....

....

....

....

....

....

....

....

....

....

Do I think that I spend the right amount of time in self-reflection? Or too much? Or too little? ....

....

....

....

....

....

....

....

....

....

In my reflections, am I able to take a compassionate view of myself, which neither totally blames myself nor totally blames others?

....

....

....

....

....

....

....

....

....

Do I overthink? Does this stop me enjoying the moment?

Have I got friends or family who will give me honest-but-kind reflections
and feedback? ....

....

....

....

....

....

....

....

....

....

....

....

....

....

....

....

....

....

....

....

....

WORKSHEET: SLEEP ROUTINE AND GRATITUDE

This is a worksheet that you might find helpful to use every night to unwind and get in the right mental state for you to drift off to sleep.

BEDTIME CHECKLIST

Before bed I will do the following to wind down:

....

....

....

....

....

....

....

Five things that I am grateful for today. (Practising gratitude is exactly that – something you need to practise. At first, it can be really hard. Think small – e.g. a delicious coffee, a seat on the bus, less homework than usual.)

....

....

....

....

....

....

Five things I am <u>proud</u> of that I did today. (*Remember, they only need to be small things, e.g. that you got up, were friendly when you didn't want to be, called your grandma.*)

....

....

....

....

....

....

....

....

....

Any things that are playing on my mind that I need to leave behind for today.

....

....

....

....

....

....

....

....

....

....

END-OF-CHAPTER REFLECTION: THE IMPACT OF MY BODY AND BEHAVIOUR ON MY FEELINGS

What good behaviour and physical habits do I have which help me with my feelings? ....
....
....
....
....
....
....
....
....

What less helpful habits do I have? ....
....
....
....
....
....
....
....
....
....

What do I do that I am <u>proud</u> of? Or what am I proud of that I avoid doing? ....

....

....

....

....

....

....

....

....

What things are more <u>difficult</u> for me to do or not do?

....

....

....

....

....

....

....

....

....

....

....

What would I like to change about my physical or behavioural habits?

....

....

....

....

....

....

....

....

....

....

....

....

....

....

....

....

PSYCHOLOGICAL TOP TIP
Changing behavioural and physiological habits is really tricky and involves motivation, willpower and repetition, repetition and more repetition. There will be much more about this in the final part of this book, Putting It All Together.

CHAPTER 6

UNDERSTANDING HOW YOUR THINKING IMPACTS ON YOUR FEELINGS

'Acknowledge your feelings to yourself, allow yourself to feel them, but don't ruminate in them. Check out reality and try to distract or move yourself on from them in a kindly way. Don't beat yourself up for feeling something but equally, don't sit with it for hours, letting it dominate. Find that emotional balance; find that emotional competence.'

There is an irrevocable link between the thoughts in your head and your mood. The power of your thoughts can trigger all those hormones and bodily responses we looked at in the previous chapter. As the famous stoic philosopher Epictetus said about 2,000 years ago: 'People are not disturbed by things, but by the view they take of them.' Changing the patterns of your thinking is key if your mood is low, anxious or angry. In this chapter, we will be looking at what you think about and how you think about it. We will also be looking at some common 'errors' in how people think, which have an impact on mood.

WHAT YOU THINK ABOUT

What do you spend your time thinking about? Using different colours or patterns, make a pie chart estimating how much of your awake time you spend thinking about the various aspects of your life:

☐ School / work

☐ Family

☐ Friends

☐ Hobbies / sports

☐ Interests

☐ Appearance

☐ Romance

☐ Health

☐ Online

☐ ....

☐ ....

☐ ....

WHAT YOU WANT TO THINK ABOUT IN THE FUTURE

Do you want to be thinking about the stuff you are thinking about?
Or do you think about some things too much or too little?
What changes would you like to make in your thinking?

On this second pie chart, look into the future and see how you'd like your
mind to be. What do you want to be thinking about?

◻ School / work   ◻ Romance
◻ Family   ◻ Health
◻ Friends   ◻ Online
◻ Hobbies / sports   ◻ ....
◻ Interests   ◻ ....
◻ Appearance   ◻ ....

REFLECTING ON WHAT YOU THINK ABOUT

PSYCHOLOGICAL TOP TIP
You can't really control what POPS into your head, but you have SOME control over what you KEEP in your head. Refocusing your attention is a skill which requires endless practice. Your mind will wander – that is what minds do – but you always have the option to refocus.

What are the differences between the two pie charts?

....

....

....

....

....

....

....

....

....

....

....

....

....

....

....

What am I thinking about now that I don't want to be thinking about in the future? ....

....

....

....

....

....

....

....

....

....

....

....

....

....

....

....

....

....

....

....

....

What new things am I thinking about (or thinking about more) in the second pie chart? How can I ensure that I do think about them more in day-to-day life? ....

....

....

....

....

....

....

....

....

....

....

....

....

....

....

....

....

....

....

....

REFLECTING ON HOW YOU THINK

Thinking isn't just about the content of your thoughts, it is also about your thinking style. This exercise is designed to help you understand your thinking style better.

Thinking about the present

1	2	3	4	5

I am just focused on pushing through with my stuff. I don't self-reflect much.	My thoughts take in the positives and negatives of the situation, and allow for nuance and shades of grey.	It's hard to focus on the present. I feel sad about the past and worry about the future.

Thinking about the future

1	2	3	4	5

I tend to be over-optimistic in what will happen. E.g. I think I'll ace a test and then I fail.	I tend to be pretty realistic about how the future will play out.	I tend to have thoughts that the worst will happen. Eg. that I'll fail a test and my life will be ruined.

Thinking about myself

```
1          2          3          4          5
●━━━━━━━━━━━━━━━━━━━━━━━━━━━━━━━━━━━━━━━━━━●
```

> My thoughts focus on my good qualities and achievements. I don't think about my faults really at all.

> Like most humans I'm neither all good nor all bad. I can keep this in mind most of the time.

> My thoughts tell me I'm an awful bad person. They focus more on my mistakes and faults.

Thinking about other people

```
1          2          3          4          5
●━━━━━━━━━━━━━━━━━━━━━━━━━━━━━━━━━━━━━━━━━━●
```

> I pay no attention to what people think of me.

> I do keep an eye on what people are thinking and feeling about me but I don't let it dominate my thinking.

> I get a lot of thoughts that people are thinking about me. I change my behaviour to try and make them think well of me.

Thinking about blame and responsibility

1   2   3   4   5

My thoughts focus on my good qualities and achievements. I don't think about my faults really at all.	Like everyone, I sometimes make mistakes. I try to take responsibility, apologise, but sometimes I blame others!	My thoughts tell me that I am to blame a lot. I tend to apologise even when things aren't my fault.

Thinking about the way I run my life

1   2   3   4   5

I don't set standards and expectations for myself. I think I should be free to do what I want when I want.	I do have some standards and expectations of myself, but I don't torture myself with them. My life isn't one long to-do list!	I have lots of rules about how I run my life. I use words like 'should' and 'must' a lot. I judge myself harshly when I don't keep them.

PSYCHOLOGICAL TOP TIP

In this exercise, thinking-in-the-middle (around a 3), realistically but compassionately, will be best for your mood, your relationships and your success. There is a belief that thinking negatively about yourself will motivate you, but research indicates the opposite is true.

Where did I fall in these continuums?

....
....
....
....
....
....
....
....
....
....
....
....
....
....
....
....
....
....
....
....
....
....
....
....
....
....

What do I think about that?

....

....

....

....

....

....

....

....

....

....

....

....

....

....

....

....

....

....

....

....

NEGATIVE AUTOMATIC THOUGHTS

Catastrophising
When things now or in the future are seen by your mind as an absolute disaster and the end of the world.

Fortune telling
When you predict the future, often in negative terms.

Emotional reasoning
I feel it, so it must be true.

**Personalisation
and mind reading**
Your head is telling you that
people are thinking or talking about
you – usually in the most
negative terms.

**Black-and-white
thinking**
When your thinking only allows
you to think that something is either
right or wrong – good or bad – and
doesn't appreciate the shades of grey.

Absolute thinking
When your thinking self-talk uses
words like <u>never</u>, <u>always</u> and <u>everyone</u>
to make overgeneralisations about
negative things happening.

**Magnifying and
minimising**
Your thinking highlights some
aspect of the situation (e.g. that you
got a D in a test) and ignores other
aspects (that you never have before).

WORKSHEET: NEGATIVE AUTOMATIC THOUGHTS

When you find yourself ruminating or overthinking about an issue, see if your thoughts are falling into any of these common (but often untrue and unhelpful) patterns. One single thought may even fall into several.

I am thinking about:

....

....

Catastrophising

Fortune telling

Emotional reasoning

Personalisation and mind reading

Black-and-white thinking

Absolute thinking

Magnifying and minimising

175

THINKING SPIRALS

Does your thinking ever spiral up? Often spiralling involves thinking error upon thinking error to an exponential growth of anxiety and panic. In my experience thinking spirals have two favourite places to go – to criticism of you, or to some irrational place where you are a failure, or excluded from everything or sometimes both! I've put an example from page 163 of *YDUM* here and a worksheet on the next page. Have you any example from your own life where this has happened?

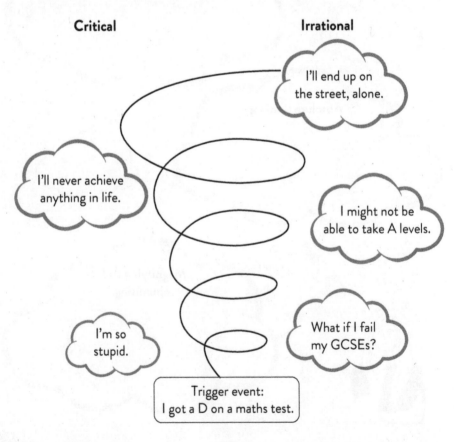

Critical

Irrational

I'll end up on the street, alone.

I'll never achieve anything in life.

I might not be able to take A levels.

I'm so stupid.

What if I fail my GCSEs?

Trigger event: I got a D on a maths test.

WORKSHEET: TRACKING YOUR THINKING SPIRAL

Is your overthinking spiralling up through thinking error to irrational or critical places?

I am thinking about: ....
....

Critical voice?

Irrational voice?

Trigger event:

Do I have thinking spirals?

....
....
....

Can I track them?

....
....
....

Do they go to self-critical?

....
....
....

Or to irrational?

....
....
....

Or both?

....
....
....

SEPARATING YOU FROM YOUR CRITICAL OR IRRATIONAL VOICE

PSYCHOLOGICAL TOP TIP

Sometimes, your critical or irrational internal voices can feel like YOU! But they are not you – they are just some thoughts in your head. To separate them from you, you can give them different names from you. That name can be something meaningful to you, e.g. someone who criticised you in the past. Or it might be completely random, like Rick and Morty or Joey and Chandler (somehow, I think Joey would be irrational and Chandler would be critical!).

Going forward, the first step in tackling these voices is then just recognising that they have arrived in your head again. 'Hello critical voice... there you are again.' Or, 'Oh, hello irrational voice – I've heard you, but please can you F*** Off now so I can get on with my life.'

What might you call your critical voice in your head? What would you like to say to it next time it shows up? ....

....

....

....

....

....

....

....

What might you call your irrational, catastrophic voice in your head? And what would you like to say to it next time? ....
....
....
....
....
....
....
....
....
....
....
....
....
....
....
....
....
....
....
....
....
....
....
....
....
....

WORKSHEET: TACKLING YOUR CRITICAL AND IRRATIONAL VOICE

What is your irrational or critical voice saying to you today?

....

....

....

....

....

....

List the reasons that this is not accurate... ....

....

....

....

....

....

List the reasons this is not helpful... ....

....

....

....

....

....

....

PSYCHOLOGICAL TOP TIP

When we challenge our thinking to live up to the standards of being accurate and helpful, we generally find a wiser way of thinking. But that wiser voice can be hard to hold on to at first; it's quiet and slips away easily and our old ways of thinking are solid and noisy (just not right or helpful!). Writing down our new wiser thoughts can make them more substantial, more real and more present. Now repeat them, share them, test them out on your best friends. Include your wiser, more accurate, more realistic voice in your life.

A wiser, more accurate and helpful way of thinking is...

....
....
....
....
....
....
....
....
....
....
....
....
....
....

END-OF-CHAPTER REFLECTION: THE IMPACT OF MY THINKING ON MY FEELINGS

I have noticed the following patterns in my thinking in this chapter...

....

....

....

....

....

....

....

....

....

....

I have noticed some thoughts that elicit difficult feelings are...

....

....

....

....

....

....

....

....

I do some helpful things with my thinking, such as...

....
....
....
....
....
....
....
....
....
....
....

I also do some unhelpful things with my thinking, such as...

....
....
....
....
....
....
....
....
....

I would like to change this pattern in my thinking by...

....

....

....

....

....

....

....

....

....

PSYCHOLOGICAL TOP TIP
If you want to change your thinking, it is a long-term commitment and often requires interrupting and distracting yourself from your inaccurate and unhelpful thinking again and again.

SELF-GROWTH: PUTTING IT ALL TOGETHER

In this part of the book, we are going to pull together everything that we have explored so far, but before we do that, I'm going to invite you to do some exercises around psychological balance. I have picked out some areas where I find a lot of young people struggle with balance. These are: comparison; work; food and eating; best-seeking and mood. Finding balance is really important in mental health, and so these exercises will help you think about the tipping point where these factors or actions can change from positive things to becoming unhelpful.

Then, we are going to look again at what your values are, what expectations you hold for yourself and think about whether these things are consistent with each other, and with your actions, to help you live a mentally healthy life. I'm also inviting you to look at your strengths.

Finally, there are two different formulation sheets to help you pull together all the information you now have about yourself. The first sheet can help you consolidate the self-knowledge and the self-reflection you've done through the workbook, which should give you insight into yourself. That might be enough for you.

But understanding yourself may not be enough: you may also want to make a change about something specific or develop personally too. Do you remember what you said you wanted to change at the beginning of the book (pages 9 and 13)? You can also use the second formulation worksheet as a springboard into the future: to think about personal growth. This might be something big about your life, or yourself, or a smaller problem. Either way, on this second formulation and the worksheets that follow, you can consider what your options are and put a plan in place.

FINDING BALANCE

PSYCHOLOGICAL TOP TIP

A lot of the problems I see come from a lack of balance in life: often from taking something which would be OK or good in moderation and doing it to an extreme.

Too much of a good thing is not a good thing. There is a tipping point where it changes into a bad thing.

These next quizzes are to check out the balance in your life. After each quiz, there is a space for self-reflection. In your reflections, think about whether this a problem area for you. If so, is it a problem because you have unrealistic expectations for yourself? Or because of the expectations of others? For example, of always 'doing better and getting more'. Remember, unrealistic expectations can be really unhelpful for mental health. On these quizzes, being in the middle around a 3 is the best place to be in terms of your mental health.

FINDING BALANCE WITH COMPARISON

General attitude to comparison

1   2   3   4   5

I don't care what other people do or say. I have my own way, and I don't value the choices of others.	I compare myself to others a bit. It's only natural to see what other people are doing.	I compare myself to others and think about what they are doing a lot.

Attitude to other people's opinions

1   2   3   4   5

I don't think much about what anyone else thinks. They're not me, why does it matter?	I care what people think about me, especially my friends, but sometimes we make different choices, and they don't always agree with mine.	I spend a lot of time thinking about what other people think about me. It's really important to me.

Beating myself up

1   2   3   4   5

When I compare myself to others, I generally think negatively of them, that they are fools.

When I compare myself, I accept that I have strengths and weaknesses and so will other people.

I will often beat myself up when I compare myself to others. I want this to motivate me to be better.

Self-deprecation

1   2   3   4   5

I don't self-deprecate. Geez, people criticise enough without criticising yourself.

I sometimes take the piss out of myself as I, like everyone, make silly mistakes and can be ridiculous at times. It's good to be able to laugh at yourself on occasion.

I often self-deprecate to manage other people's expectations of me or so I don't seem big-headed.

Admiration

1   2   3   4   5

I don't care much about the good opinion of others. I am my own person and they are not going to agree with my choices.	I like it if people think well of me, and I feel a bit perturbed when they don't, but you can't please everyone. We are all different.	I want everyone I meet to think well of me and act in ways so that they will admire me or think I'm impressive.

Afterwards

Seeking reassurance and explaining

1   2   3   4   5

Either I don't care if I've upset someone or if I do care, I will try to blame them.	Generally, I know I am a good friend, but if I make a mistake, l will talk it over with a friend or apologise.	I often worry afterwards about what I said or did or what people thought about me. I might seek reassurance or go back and try to explain it.

Fitting in/ belonging

```
●————————————————————————————————————————————————————●
1               2               3               4               5
```

| I don't have much of a sense of belonging or fitting in, or there are a few people I hang with, but we are on the sides of the main group. | I have my own friendship group and I feel like I belong. I don't feel like I have to compete or compare myself to my friends. | I worry about fitting in my friendship group. I want to be one of the best in the group, so I feel secure of my place. |

PSYCHOLOGICAL TOP TIP

Having a balanced approach to comparison is best: caring neither too much nor too little. Many young women I see get caught in a comparison trap: they compare themselves a lot, because they want to be part of the group, but also because they want to be admired and seen as better. This is a no-win situation: you cannot be both the same and better! Comparison and competition also act to keep people at a distance, either through a lack of honest vulnerability or through friends sensing it and finding it off-putting.

Reflections on my relationship with comparison:

....

....

....

....

....

....

....

....

....

....

....

....

....

....

....

....

....

....

....

....

....

FINDING BALANCE WITH YOUR WORK

General attitude to work

1   2   3   4   5

I tend not to think too much about my work, which means sometimes I don't do as well as I should or get in trouble for not doing it.	I work reasonably hard and get most of my work done vaguely on time and to a good enough standard.	My work dominates my life and I arrange everything else around it. I work very hard, and try to do every piece to the best of my ability.

Procrastination-avoidance

1   2   3   4   5

Sometimes I procrastinate as work is so boring and I just want to do other stuff. I can't face it.	I tend to just get work done as quickly and efficiently as possible so I can get on with having fun.	I feel compelled to start work or make a plan about when I do, as I can't relax with it hanging over me.

Perfection

1   2   3   4   5

I don't care much about the standard of my work, I just need to avoid getting into trouble.	I like my work to be good but I'm not going to waste hours and hours trying to get every last bit right.	I go over and over work or can't stop working till I feel I have every detail right. I usually don't feel like it's good enough, so I can't relax.

Perfection-procrastination

1   2   3   4   5

I procrastinate a lot both before I start and while I'm doing my work. I can end up submitting work I know isn't good enough.	Sometimes I procrastinate, but not because I feel my work needs to be perfect! I finish when it's good enough or I have something more important to do.	I struggle to stop working on something, as I'm trying to make it perfect. That means sometimes I am reluctant to start work as once I start it, I won't be able to stop working until the deadline.

Test and exam results

1   2   3   4   5

| I don't get very good grades generally. | I get a mixture of results. Sometimes I do well, sometimes I do less well. | I generally achieve A or A* and feel people expect that of me. My results don't give me much joy, but I would feel devastated if I didn't do well. |

Timing of work

1   2   3   4   5

| Sometimes I work late into the night because I didn't start till late as I was faffing around. | I usually just finish working when I get tired or when I know it's my bedtime. | Sometimes I work too late into the night as I'm trying to improve or perfect something. |

Work and the future

1   2   3   4   5

| The amount of work I do may impact on my future life options. | I will probably achieve vaguely what I want in life. | I could probably work less hard and achieve what I want in life. |

PSYCHOLOGICAL TOP TIP

Having a balanced approach to work is best, and emotional intelligence and good mental health are linked to future success, so it is counterproductive to push yourself too hard. Societal glorification of hard work leads many young people to become deeply unhappy.

At the other extreme, not doing much work at all will limit your life options.

Reflections on my attitude to work:

....
....
....
....
....
....
....
....
....
....
....
....
....
....
....
....
....
....
....
....
....
....

FINDING BALANCE WITH FOOD, EATING, WEIGHT AND SHAPE

General attitude to weight and shape

1   2   3   4   5

| I don't care at all about my shape and weight. | I care a bit about my shape and weight, but it's only one thing about my appearance and generally people make too much fuss over appearance anyway. | I think about my shape or weight all the time. I really want to be thin. |

General attitude to food and eating

1   2   3   4   5

| I regularly eat much more than I need. Often I feel uncomfortably full. | I generally eat what I want and eat all food types. I keep a vague eye on nutrition. | I eat a very 'healthy' diet, focusing onlow-fat, low-sugar and/or low-carb foods. I rarely or never have fast or snack foods. |

Overeating/ dieting

1   2   3   4   5

I eat exactly what I want when I want it, and often that means I'm eating fast food or snack food.	I tend to stop eating when I am full. I try not to overeat but don't diet.	I am always on a diet with food rules about the type, amount or timing of foods.

Weight gain/ loss/ staying the same (this question isn't relevant if you are going through puberty or still growing (up to age 18–20) as your weight should still be increasing).

1   2   3   4   5

Even though I've stopped growing, my weight goes up every year.	Since I finished growing and puberty, my weight stays about the same.	I'm always trying to lose weight.

'What the hell' eating

1   2   3   4   5

Sometimes I think 'what the hell' and eat a very large amount of food.	I don't ever really eat much too much food, except perhaps on Christmas Day or other celebration days.	If I break my diet, I tend to think 'what the hell, I've ruined it for the day and may as well eat all the things I normally don't'.

Exercise and movement

1   2   3   4   5

I don't exercise or move my body very much.	I exercise for fun or for physical or mental health reasons.	I exercise to stay in shape and burn calories.

PSYCHOLOGICAL TOP TIP

As I said earlier in Chapter 5, not eating enough will mess with your mood and ultimately your mental health. Dieting is linked to both future eating disorders and obesity and should be avoided. Eating with family and friends, getting a good balance between intuition (what you fancy) and nutrition (what your body needs) and stopping when you are full, are all signs of psychologically healthy eating (*YDUM* pg.246).

Reflections on food, eating, weight and shape:

....

....

....

....

....

....

....

....

....

....

....

....

....

....

FINDING BALANCE WITH BEST-SEEKING

Doing my best

1   2   3   4   5

| I don't care about doing well. | I try hard but I'm not really competing with anyone except myself. I'm on my own path. | I think it is important to do my best in every area of my life all the time. |

Getting the best

1   2   3   4   5

| I have very little personal ambition at the moment. | I choose universities, courses and jobs based on whether or not they suit me, not what other people think. | It's important to me to get into a prestigious university or course, and to aim for the 'top' jobs and the 'top' firms. |

Other people's opinions

1 2 3 4 5

| I don't think much about what people think about me, or I just expect they think I'm a loser. | I like to be thought of well, but ultimately I can't control what other people think of me. | I want other people to see that I'm one of the best or brightest. |

Multiple domains (e.g. appearance, work, social or family relationships, hobbies like music or sport)

1 2 3 4 5

| I don't expect to do well in any areas of life. | I care about how I do in one or two areas of my life, but not really any of the others. | I want to be the best in several areas of life. |

Never satisfied?

1   2   3   4   5

I don't feel satisfied with myself but I don't feel engaged in trying to change that either.	I'm good enough! I try hard but I don't beat myself up about my faults or failures.	I am rarely completely satisfied with myself – if I achieve in one area of my life, I often feel bad that I've been neglecting another area.

PSYCHOLOGICAL TOP TIP

Another word for 'best-seeking' is perfectionism, but I have met hundreds of perfectionists in my clinics and they rarely identify with this term, because clearly (they think!), they are nowhere near perfect. They just want to be the best, and get everything right, and be liked by everyone in everything they do! This is exactly what perfectionism is, but I'm calling it best-seeking, as I think it better catches my patients' mentality.

So, best-seeking (or perfectionism) is a relentless seeking of higher and higher standards in most areas of life, with a belief that happiness will come through achieving those standards. Best-seekers never feel like they are good enough as there is always room for self-improvement. This way of living life is associated with mental illness, disconnection and burnout – not success.

Reflections on best-seeking:

....
....
....
....
....
....
....
....
....
....
....
....
....
....
....
....
....
....
....
....
....
....
....
....
....
....

FINDING BALANCE WITH MY MOOD

Frequency of mood disorder

1   2   3   4   5

I get very strong feelings a lot. I often feel overwhelmed by them.	I get very strong feelings on occasion and sometimes I feel overwhelmed by them.	I get very strong feelings a lot. I often feel overwhelmed by them.

Mood management

1   2   3   4   5

I often feel so desperate in my mood, I do destructive things. I might try to numb it with drugs, alcohol, self-harm or similar.	When I feel low in my mood, I try to get out of it by talking to someone or taking care of myself.	I feel so desperate to avoid difficult moods, I make plans, routines or rituals to try to control the situation.

Avoiding things

1   2   3   4   5

I often avoid doing things that will make me feel better or getting on with core life tasks like work or self-care.	I basically do most things I should although sometimes, like everyone, I cba in my self-care or work.	I avoid social situations or want to leave, as I feel a bit out of control. I plan out my work and responsibilities.

Spontaneity and uncertainty

1   2   3   4   5

I feel out of control a lot of the time. I often do things which make me feel more out of control.	I try to keep vaguely organised and on task, but also accept that life is uncertain and that good or bad things happen out of the blue. Some of the fun in life comes spontaneously!	I hate the feeling that I am out of control of something. I strive to be in control all the time. I plan out my life meticulously.

Openness

1   2   3   4   5

I talk very freely about my mood, and so most people know that I am struggling.	I share any mood problems with close friends and family, but not with everyone I meet.	People see me as very controlled and organised. Most people don't know I'm struggling, although I may seek reassurance.

Identity

1   2   3   4   5

I see my mood difficulties as intrinsic to the person I am. I can't see that ever changing.	When I struggle with my mood, I see it as part of me, but not my key identity.	I see control and organisation as key to my personality.

PSYCHOLOGICAL TOP TIP

Your difficult feelings may not be your fault, but they are your responsibility.

Doing negative and destructive things on the one end of the continuum, or avoiding and controlling on the other end of the continuum, may give you short-term relief from difficult feelings, but both will likely make the problem worse in the long term.

Feelings are data from your body to make wise decisions, not dictates to be indulged, numbed or an excuse for bad behaviour.

Feelings need to be felt: acknowledged and thought about, learnt from.

However, if you find that you can't manage them with positive coping strategies, you may need to seek medical or professional help. That is a different way of taking responsibility, which has no shame or blame attached. Sometimes feelings are just too hard or too strong.

Reflections on finding balance with my mood:

....

....

....

....

....

....

....

....

....

VALUES

At the beginning of this book, I asked you to pick five values that reflect how you want to live your life. I'm going to ask you to do this again without looking back (ignore the shading for now).

Academic achievement		Admiration	
Adventure		Ambition	
Authenticity		Competition	
Belonging		Career	
Caring/ self-care		Compassion	
Confidence		Connection	
Contentment		Control	
Creativity		Curiosity	
Diversity		Environment	
Equality		Excellence	
Faith		Family	
Financial stability		Freedom	
Friendship		Fun	
Gratitude		Health and Fitness	
Home		Honesty	
Hope		Humour	
Inclusion		Independence	

Industry		Integrity	
Intimacy		Joy	
Kindness		Leisure	
Love		Making a difference	
Mindfulness		Nature	
Openness		Optimism	
Order		Peace	
Persistence and commitment		Power	
Pride		Responsibility	
Risk-taking		Safety	
Self-discipline		Sportsmanship	
Success		Trustworthy	
Uniqueness		Work–life balance	

Reflections on your values

Looking back at my values on pages 18–19 at the start of this book, have they changed over the course of the book? (*Neither is right or wrong, but it might be interesting to you.*)

....

....

....

....

....

....

....

....

Are my values consistent with one another or do they clash? Were they consistent at the start of the book?

....

....

....

....

....

....

....

....

....

Do my day-to-day thoughts, feelings and behaviour actually match the values I've identified here?

....

....

....

....

....

....

....

....

....

What would I need to do more or less of to make them match better?

....

....

....

....

....

....

....

....

....

How many of my five values were shaded on the Values list?

....

....

....

....

....

....

....

....

....

....

....

....

PSYCHOLOGICAL TOP TIP

Any of these values taken to extreme can become a problem. For example, faith taken to extreme can lead to acts of terrorism and war. However, more prosaically, the values in grey are the values that I see most often taken to extreme and can lead young people to mental distress and mental illness. These are the values that can lead to people to seek too much 'best-seeking' which as we have seen is really bad for you. *YDUM* has much more on this. Have you ticked too many of these?

How do your values fit with your future life plans? Are they consistent with your future study, work or relationship choices?

....
....
....
....
....
....
....
....
....
....
....
....
....
....
....
....
....
....
....
....

EXPECTATIONS

Throughout this book, I've encouraged you to look at the expectations that other people, institutions, society, situations and you, yourself, put on you. As we near the end of the book, I want to ask you to list here all the expectations, rules, 'shoulds' and 'musts' you have found you live under. Listing them all in one place may help you think about whether these are all realistic expectations to keep, e.g. are there too many? Are they contradictory?

....

....

....

....

....

....

....

....

....

....

....

....

....

....

....

....

....

....

....

....

....

....

....

....

....

....

....

....

....

....

....

PSYCHOLOGICAL TOP TIP

I see too many young women juggling with too many expectations, and you know what happens when you juggle with too much? You drop stuff. Look back at your values and align your expectations to run with these values. You may need to set yourself free from other people's expectations that don't matter to you, or from your own expectations which are keeping you caged in or miserable.

What expectations do I want to keep? Which ones do I most urgently need to let go of?

....
....
....
....
....
....
....
....
....
....
....
....
....
....
....
....
....
....
....
....
....

MY STRENGTHS

By now you probably know yourself pretty well: we've thought about your family, friends, life circumstances and events. You've looked inside yourself and examined your feelings and also the things that you do that help you and things that you do that don't. You've considered your thinking patterns.

I hope you've been compassionate to yourself all the way through. Now, here is an extra chance for kindness. I want you to write about your own strengths. Pretend you are writing your own yearbook entry, as they focus only on the positives. Yearbooks just interview people who like you, get you, think you're funny, cool, smart. They tell of your successes and achievements and kindnesses done. Please do this for yourself, without any caveats or criticism – just your strengths and positives.

....

....

....

....

....

....

....

....

....

....

....

....

....
....
....
....
....
....
....
....
....
....
....

If I was summarising my strengths, I would say they are...

....
....
....
....
....
....
....
....
....
....
....
....

PUTTING IT ALL TOGETHER: UNDERSTANDING YOURSELF

When our emotions are strong, when we feel stuck or when we are not sure what to do, it is hard to think clearly. Sometimes in psychology, we use a formulation to help us capture what is going on. On the next two pages are photocopiable blank formulation worksheets to help you.

The first of these is to pull together the self-knowledge and self-reflection to help you understand yourself in any situation. The second formulation sheet expands on the first but also creates options in moving forwards: opportunities for change and growth. The second one may be more suitable when you are facing a problem where you need to do something.

You may wish to return to these sheets again and again. As you go back to them, you may notice patterns of similarities and differences in your background factors, trigger events or thoughts. These may give you other ideas about things you need to change in the longer term.

WORKSHEET: PUTTING IT ALL TOGETHER: UNDERSTANDING YOURSELF

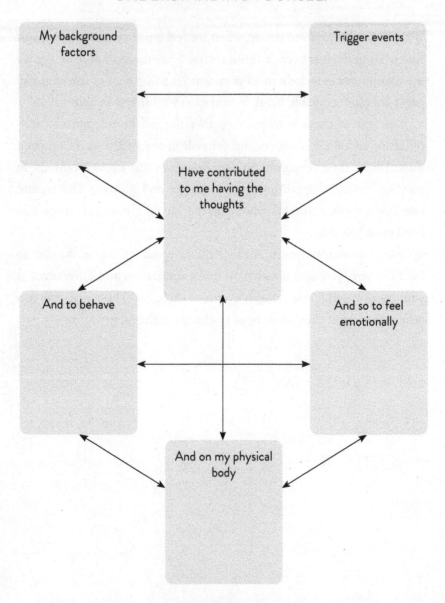

My background factors

Trigger events

Have contributed to me having the thoughts

And to behave

And so to feel emotionally

And on my physical body

WORKSHEET: PUTTING IT ALL TOGETHER: UNDER-STANDING YOURSELF AND OPTIONS FOR CHANGE

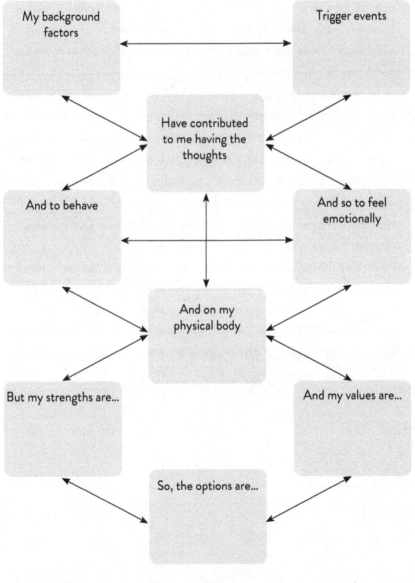

PSYCHOLOGICAL TOP TIP

If you have a difficult problem to solve or life decision to make, it's a good idea to write down all the possible options, even the ones that seem silly and that you already think you won't move forward with. Why? There are a couple of reasons why writing them down is a good idea.

Sometimes, it is hard to make a decision because there are no good or obvious options. Sometimes, decisions are about choosing the least-worst option, and in that situation your brain will go round and round, trying to find another idea. Knowing there is not another option will help you commit to the decision you made, and not make you doubt yourself. Writing them down and thinking about the pros and cons of all the options, we allow for them to be fully dismissed. Our minds will then let them go, and we gain mental peace.

Writing down your reasoning for a decision can also be useful when you are trying to change something that is counterintuitive for you, or that goes against expectations. For example, if you know you are working too hard and need to have more relaxation or fun times, writing down the pros of that option, and the cons of working too hard, can keep your reasoning in mind.

WORKSHEET: CONSIDERING MY OPTIONS

What are ALL the options?	Pro of that option	Con of that option

COMMITMENT TO GROWTH

Once you know what your options are, the right thing to do may be easy, or it may be harder and something that you need to work towards. Sometimes, you need to set a goal and break your goal down into steps. You will be more likely to succeed if you have a plan. Remember, goals don't have to always be about 'doing better and getting more'. Many of you will have more happiness and success by doing less work and having more fun, so this exercise is definitely not just the sort of outcome-based goal that you might have in school or work, e.g. to pass a test, or get an A. This is a goal for your own personal growth and so it may be to give up areas of best-seeking, or to commit to yourself to be more in the moment. It is not about what anyone else wants for your life – no one else's expectations should show up here.

WORKSHEET: COMMITMENT TO GROWTH

- Specifically, what is your goal? ....
....
....

- Is it a goal that needs to be broken down into smaller steps? If so, what is the first step to your goal? ....
....
....

- When are you going to do this by? ....
....
....

- How many times are you going to try starting or stopping it?
....
....

- When you try to start or stop any new behaviour, there are likely to be failures and setbacks. What is your strategy for when it doesn't work? ....
....
....

After you have tried starting or stopping a new behaviour, journal how that is going.

Date: ....
....
....

Date: ....
....
....

Date: ....
....
....

Date: ....
....
....

Date: ....
....
....

LAST WORDS

So, what have we learnt? What do I want you to remember so that you maximise your chances for mental wellness? I want you to remember that you get to be your own person: you don't have to live according to what your friends, family or lovers think. Rather than trying to do your best, be your truest self. Who you are inside matters more than what you look like or how good your outcomes are. You are not a product to be moulded by society's or other people's expectations. Know your own values and, within reason, try to live according to them. Know that it's impossible to hold all the values, because being perfect is a dangerous myth: it's a myth that, if you subscribe to it, will in all likelihood harm your mental health.

I want you to understand the importance of vulnerability, empathy and connection, and that comparison, competition and perfection are their enemies. Connection is made by the way you feel when you are with people and not by being the best person. Find people who make you feel good and gently drop the ones who don't. And don't confuse lust or excitement with love.

Don't forget the boring stuff: eat enough, sleep enough and move your body. Avoid extremes – nearly always, mental health is about balance and the middle road is the one with the best chance. Your feelings are like the waves in the sea: they will go up and they will go down. Like the waves, they need to be respected and you mustn't let them drown you.

Don't be too wedded to your emotional mind; let your rational mind in. Make wise choices using both.

Being vulnerable doesn't mean being a victim. Wise choices are sometimes letting go and walking away and giving up. Being scared or frightened is sometimes necessary and being sad inevitable if you want to live and love. Sometimes there will be times when you are alone and a bit lonely, and while it's OK to be a little scared of that, hold your values tight, keep offering empathy, vulnerability and connection and you will be alright.

Good luck to you, my young friend – be brave.

These last words are adapted from *You Don't Understand Me: The Young Woman's Guide to Life.*

ACKNOWLEDGEMENTS

Firstly, this journal would never have been written without the bravery of my current and former patients who, at some of their lowest points, took their courage in their hands and came to talk to a stranger about it. I learnt some stuff at school and university, but I learnt much more sitting, listening and struggling through it with you. Thank you for sharing your pain and difficulties with me.

Thank you to my dear friend and colleague Cynthia Rousso, who first suggested the idea of a journal to accompany *You Don't Understand Me*, then tirelessly suggested ideas and gave me feedback that was often annoyingly right. So many opportunities for growth! Thank you for all your support.

Also, thank you to my wonderful former colleagues from the Royal Free CAMHS clinical psychology team: Jade Ambridge, Luca Farkas, Ruhina Ladha, Jo Myers and Kate Pryce, and Sonia Wogan from the psychotherapy team. I learnt so much from you all when I worked with you and your brainstorming and insights were invaluable on this project. I really appreciated your sensitive feedback, and the book is better because of your comments.

Thank you, too, to my young readers: Bea Ayres; Paloma Eskinazi-Nehme and Carla Tenthorey-Vinuesa. Your eagle eyes spotted things seasoned professionals in therapy and publishing didn't! Your feedback was so helpful in giving me confidence that I was on the right track, and I am so grateful for you giving your time and ideas. They were incredibly helpful. Thank you, too, to Claudia Fussell for sharing her excellent journaling ideas with me.

Thank you to my agent, Victoria Hobbs, for her enthusiasm for the project and having my back.

Thank you too, to my editors, Michelle Signore and Madiya Altaf at Bonnier Books, for seeing the potential and their thoughtfulness towards it, and Susan Pegg, copyeditor, whose seemingly simple questions really nailed some key issues that needed sorting.

REFERENCES AND FURTHER INFORMATION

P.23, 49, 67, 85, 119, 161 Epigraph

All the epigraphs at the start of the chapters are from my book, *You Don't Understand Me: A Young Woman's Guide to Life*, Bonnier Books UK, 2022.

HOW TO USE THIS BOOK

P.37 Mo Gawdat, a famous author and founder of One Billion Happy.

For all things Mo Gawdat, see his website: https://www.mogawdat. com. He has books and his own podcast, and regularly appears on other podcasts. Like Kristen Neff, his own story is both heart-breaking and inspiring. Listen at: https://drchatterjee.com/bitesize-how-to-become-happier-today-mo-gawdat

CHAPTER 2

P.50 Three ways you can feel in your friendships are...

For more on fitting in versus belonging, see Brené Brown, *Atlas of the Heart*, Ebury Publishing, 2021.

CHAPTER 4

P.86 In my therapy room, I often use a feelings wheel to help people do this.

To create the feelings wheel I was influenced by the following:
- Brené Brown's analysis and deconstruction of feelings found in *Atlas of the Heart*, Ebury Publishing, 2021.
- The Buddhist concept of vedanā, which means 'feeling tone'. This is a good introduction: https://www.tenpercent.com/tph/podcast-episode/christina-feldman-500
- Gasper, K., Spencer, L.A. and Hu. D. (2019) 'Does Neutral Affect Exist? How Challenging Three Beliefs about Neutral Affect can Advance Research', *Frontiers in Psychology*, 10, 2476.

CHAPTER 5

P.126 Practise progressive muscle relaxation exercises or meditation.

Relaxation and Meditation links. There are many relaxation and mindful apps such as Calm, Headspace and Aura (which is free). I like Ten Percent Happier, which offers some free content via their podcast alongside paid content. Kristin Neff offers a lot of free guided meditations via her compassion-based website: https://self-compassion.org/category/exercises/#exercises
As does: https://www.freemindfulness.org

CHAPTER 6

P 172 These thinking patterns are called Negative Automatic Thoughts (NATs) in psychology.

If you are looking for them online, they are also sometimes called Automatic Negative Thoughts (ANTs).

'The 21st-Century Girl's Survival Pack' – **Caitlin Moran**

'I would recommend this brilliantly clear and informative book to every young girl... Tara writes with deep knowledge, warmth and humour about all the challenges young girls and all of us face, and she tells us how to overcome them.' – **Julia Samuel**

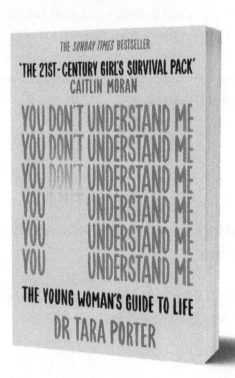

Writing directly to girls and young women Dr Tara Porter draws on decades of experience to offer them insight into their own psychology. From exams to friendship, from families to love, Tara pulls together everything she has learnt to provide accessible explanations and suggestions for teenagers and young women everywhere. Like a warm letter from a wise friend or big sister, *You Don't Understand Me* not only understands the young person's perspectives but guides them through their challenges they face.